Major Edis

Tales of Lonewater Farm

New Brunswick's
Home for Alcoholics

NIMBUS
PUBLISHING

Nimbus Publishing Ltd.
PO Box 9301, Station A
Halifax, NS B3K 5N5
(902) 455-4286

Design: Joan Sinclair

Canadian Cataloguing in Publication Data
Flewwelling, Edis A.
Major Edis A. Flewwelling and tales of Lonewater Farm
ISBN 1-55109-266-2
1. Lonewater Farm (N.B.) — History.
2. Alcoholics — Rehabilitation — New Brunswick —History.
I. Title.

RC564.75.C3F53 1998 362.292'86'09715 C98-950057-8

Printed in Canada

Nimbus acknowledges the financial assistance of the Canada Council and the Department of Canadian Heritage.

CONTENTS

ACKNOWLEDGEMENTS

Behind every book is a team. The team behind this one has been endlessly supportive and helpful; my thanks goes to all of them.

To Jim Mason for his research, to Mia Tarvis for editing, to Yvonne Wilson for her decisive editorial insight and astute comments, to Lucy Wilson for her typesetting, and clarifications, to Elizabeth Margaris for her consistent encouragement and to my dear wife Jane for her work on the final draft.

E.A.F.

DEDICATION

This book is dedicated to the men who passed through the doors of Lonewater Farm—to their efforts, their successes and their dreams.

In remembering the good times and also the strife associated with alcohol, let us not forget the bond of friendship that was created by our mutual sense of community.

Walk tall and keep smiling.

They came to Lonewater Farm,
downtrodden and ill, chronic alcoholics
looking for freedom from their addiction.
At Lonewater Farm, these men worked
and laughed their way from alcohol dependence
to renewed self-respect and hope.

FOREWORD

Many things in life can be enjoyable, even good for us, when used in moderation, but can cause us great trouble if they are abused.

Alcohol is the classic example of this. A glass of wine with dinner can be a pleasant addition to a convivial evening, relaxing us and adding to our sense of well-being. Studies show that regular moderate consumption of red wine is good for our health. But sometimes alcohol takes control, and rather than adding to our well-being, it begins to steal it away.

Alcoholics lose control over their lives, their activities. Their health, their families, their jobs are affected, often lost. Many lose their lives.

Places like Lonewater Farm are designed to try to help alcoholics recover control. Just as what makes someone an alcoholic varies from one case to another, what can help them recover also varies. There seems to be no treatment that is effective in every case, so, naturally, treatments go in and out of fashion. Presently, alcoholism is considered a disease, to be treated with medicine and therapy—effective in many cases, but not all. That is the approach used nowadays at Lonewater Farm.

This book tells the story of a different approach.

One of the worst things that alcoholism steals from its victims is their self-esteem. They have messed up their lives, lost their jobs, lost everything that might once have been important to them, including family. They feel they can do nothing right.

They feel worthless. When they dry out, they don't know how to cope with day to day life and all its little responsibilities, let alone get back all they have lost. So they drink again.

When Major Edis Flewwelling took over the newly-established Lonewater Farm treatment facility in 1968, he instituted an approach to treating alcoholism that dealt with this core problem. He wanted to help the men earn back their own sense of self-worth, and prepare them for independent life. He knew he had to take care of most things for them, so that they could gradually learn to take responsibility, without being overwhelmed by having to cope with everything all at once. But he also knew that, gradually or not, they did have to learn to be responsible for themselves.

He used a good old-fashioned method: hard work. Put the men in healthy surroundings, and let them do useful work. Let them take responsibility for their own work. Let them see that what they do helps out everyone in the group. Hard work gave them a reason to get up in the morning, a reason to have a good appetite, a reason to sleep well at night, and a reason to feel good about themselves.

The men's surroundings also helped. What better place to regain your self-worth than in an area of such natural beauty as the Lower St. John River valley? As the men were re-awakened to themselves and their world, they had only to look around to see that the world we live in is a pretty good place after all.

Whether it was the ducks arriving in the spring, the blazing colour of the trees in the fall, or even the intense blue of the sky on those bone-chilling days in January, the natural world was all around them, bringing them out of themselves, and showing them that they are part of something wonderful.

Gradually the men learned to function within the structure provided by the Farm, until they were ready to go out on their own again. Oh, not all of them succeeded—some came back several times, others just "came to a bad end." But most were helped by their time at the Farm.

This treatment style is out of fashion here now, but its time will come again. After all, lately we have been hearing occasionally of successful drug and alcohol treatment programs in other countries, and the "innovative new methods" they use. What methods? Hard work, in healthy surroundings. Give people back their sense of self-worth and responsibility

This book is the Major's memorial to the men who lived and worked with him at Lonewater Farm. It is a volume of reminiscences, not a formal history or a word-for-word reporting of events, but it is factual. Documentation exists for all of the episodes recounted here. The stories are sometimes "funny, pathetic, and exasperating"—and sometimes joyful. Although the Major's "walking wounded" did not all recover, many did. We are privileged to be able to share in their experiences.

Lucy Wilson
Oak Point, N.B.

CHAPTER ONE

The Army of Walking Wounded

NOT FAR FROM THE MOUTH OF THE ST. JOHN, just where the river bends for its final run to the sea, a beautiful stream joins in: the Nerepis.

When Europeans (mostly Americans in the 1780s) came to this country and carved it into private holdings, they also changed most of the names, but Nerepis escaped. They parcelled out her banks, dredged channels in her marshes, and cut down her trees, but they didn't change her name.

One of the first landholders along the Nerepis was a Captain Glasier (various spellings exist); another was Major (later General) John Coffin. Captain Glasier came from England in 1765, sent out to help secure the area against a possible American war. Major Coffin was a Loyalist. Having arrived ahead of the inflow of settlers from the States, Captain Glasier faced little competition for the best land and chose the Nerepis valley; he had a grant authorizing 5,000 acres and bought 1,000 more. Major Coffin, too late for the best site, settled nearby at Beaubear's Point (now Woodman's Point).

Shortly after the Major took up his holding, Captain Glasier and Major Coffin took the same ship for England. Before they reached port, Captain Glasier was dead and Major Coffin owned 6,000 acres on the Nerepis. There was no bill of sale (only the deeds to the property) and gossip whispered of a poker game, but nobody questioned the Major's right to the land. No doubt they wouldn't; he must have been a hard man.

One day when Major Coffin and his family had not been long at Beaubear's Point, he set out for Saint John by rowboat, his little daughter perched in the bow. That was 12 miles away, by river! It is unlikely that the Major himself was doing the rowing.

As they were rowing along, a bear, which had been terrorizing cattle by the river and had been chased away by farmhands, in its panic rushed into the water and struck out straight for the boat.

“Do not scream, child,” the Major ordered, and (like father, like daughter, or just scared out of her wits) the child did not scream. She held her peace until the bear’s paw rested on the boat, at which point the Major raised an oar and struck it dead. Then the little girl set up a howl and the villagers near the bank gathered to find out what was going on.

Having disposed of the bear by arranging for some of the men to tow the carcass to his house, the Major proceeded on his way. He didn’t even mention the incident to his friends in town. His deportment was a credit to his family, whose motto was “In Tempestate Floresco / We thrive in adversity.”

There are still bears to be encountered along the Nerepis, as recent residents relate in this narrative. The Coffin family, however, has moved on. Major Coffin deeded part of his estate to his son John Townshend Coffin, who took up residence in the family home in 1832. It came to be called the Manor House.

John Townshend Coffin sold the property to Robert F. Hazen who named the place Lonewater Farm, an appropriate name for a holding that stood in the wilds of southern New Brunswick and could be reached only by boat.

Time passed and owners came and went, but Lonewater, like the river, retained its name.

In the 1780s, when looking for a place to settle, Edward Winslow wrote of the Nerepis valley, “It is the pleasantest part of the country and I am sure that the land is better than any I have ever seen.” In the 1980s another citizen looking for land to develop turned fairly green with envy when he saw Lonewater Farm. “What a holiday resort this place would make!” he cried. But that was not exactly its destiny.

The future will unfold, as the Loyalist past did. This account deals with the years between my appointment as manager of Lonewater Farm in the autumn of 1968 and my retirement, December 1986.

IN OCTOBER 1976, a six-page booklet describing "a project of the residents of Lonewater Farm at Westfield, a rural alcoholic rehabilitation facility ... designed to acquaint the public with the aims and purposes of the facility and some of its aspirations for the future," was written, printed, and bound, ready for distribution.

The residents of that day saw Lonewater Farm as "a rural retreat where alcoholics could work their way back to health and self-respect...."

"... Lonewater Farm does not pretend to be a panacea for alcoholism—most likely none exists—" the little publication went on to say, "but the fact remains that hundreds of arrested alcoholics are living productive lives today because of a stay at the Farm, perhaps one of the most valuable institutions in New Brunswick today.... As for admission, generally speaking, it's open to any man who has been treated for alcoholism and who no longer requires hospital treatment."

On page three of their booklet, the residents wrote:

"Major Edis Flewwelling, who has managed the farm since its inception, is the first to admit that the operation is far from perfect and has had its share of failures. Statistics are hard to come by: some [men] leave the farm, do well but leave the area and aren't heard from again; others return to their highly visible existences on the city's street corners.

"But it's the successes—the men who give up the jug for good—that make the whole thing worthwhile," says the Major. He estimates that the success rate at Lonewater Farm is roughly comparable to that of any other rehabilitation centre in Canada.

"Numerous ex-residents, who once arrived in rags, visit the farm, often along with their reunited families and sporting good clothes and responsible jobs. They're welcomed with open arms and a good meal.

"The important thing about Lonewater Farm, say residents and management alike, is that it offers the suffering alcoholic a second chance in life—another crack at the whip. Whether or not he takes advantage of this opportunity is strictly up to him."

The booklet continues, "The residents of Lonewater Farm—they're never called patients, inmates or any of the other euphemisms for denizens of institutions—come from all walks of life. There are professional and businessmen, clerks and bus-boys, tradesmen and labourers, and their combined labour has enabled the farm to expand physically and to become at least partially self-supporting through sale of pulpwood and other commodities and services rented out to residents of the sur-rounding countryside.

"With 27 years' military service behind him, Major Flewwelling has a sound relationship with the residents, but he brooks no nonsense—any man who drinks on the farm or tries to smuggle in booze after a visit to town is quickly shown the exit gate. But that doesn't mean the same man won't get another chance at a later date if his attitude changes and he shows a genuine desire to shuck the hooch for good.

"... While this philosophy of instilling pride in this army of reforming drunks by honest and dignified (if sometimes hum-ble) labour has had considerable success over the years, not every guest at the farm is sincere in his desire to quit drinking and there have been spectacular failures.

"As Major Flewwelling puts it, 'If the basic desire to stop drinking isn't there, there's very little we, or anyone else, can do for a man.' " ("Lonewater Farm," Oct. 1976.)

IN THE FALL OF 1967, Dr. Jack McLaughlin, Director of the Alcoholic Ward at the Provincial Hospital, realized that there were more men out on the street suffering from alcoholism than his ward could handle. Especially in bad weather, the police might bring in a patient at any hour of the day or night, and all the beds would be taken.

The question the ward staff would then have to ask one another was, who has been here the longest?

A search of the records would soon come up with a name, and that person would have to leave, return to the streets, to make room for the new arrival, even though he might have been in the hospital a very short time.

The doctor felt he had to do something about this situation.

As he lived in Westfield, one of the western suburbs of Saint John, he knew the area around Woodman's Point, and he thought of Lonewater Farm. Lonewater might possibly be for sale, he thought; and if he could buy it, he would. Then, if he could procure help from the Province, he would set up the place as a rehabilitation centre for alcoholics.

One evening he drove to the farm and put his proposition before the owner, a woman the residents later called Annie because she reminded them of Tugboat Annie. Dr. McLaughlin offered Annie his best price, but she wanted $10,000 more than he could take from his own pocket.

The doctor was not prepared to go into debt for the property, but he did not give up his idea. He talked to Dr. Gregory, the Director of the Hospital, and suggested to him that together they should approach the Department of Health and see if they could talk the Province into buying the farm.

Much to the doctor's gratification, the Province was interested. Representatives of the Department accompanied them on another visit to Annie, and agreement was reached—even though Annie raised the price another $35,000 when she found that the government would be the buyer.

The project was moving ahead much faster than anyone could have predicted. Even in the expansive sixties, fiscal restraints were real and limiting, and the Province could not buy the property until the 1968 budget had been approved. The Department of Health, therefore, arranged to rent the farm in the interim; and Annie agreed to stay on as temporary caretaker, though she had an apartment in Halifax where she usually lived, keeping the farm only for occasional holidays.

A man from the staff of the Provincial Hospital was assigned to act as liaison with the hospital and to give Annie a hand; he bought groceries and delivered them to the farm, for example. Dr. McLaughlin sent up three or four patients to look after the animals: three cows and a few goats and chickens, and to start cleaning up the place and making it ready for as many residents as the buildings could accommodate; besides the main house (the Manor House) there were the farm house, a cottage, a barn, and several outbuildings. Before long, the street alcoholics of the city became aware that there was now a place where a man, prepared to forego the bottle and to work for his keep, could find shelter for the coming winter.

It was not yet the end of the first year! Only November. Just a few months from the day Dr. McLaughlin had first proposed his idea, and Lonewater Farm was already beginning to function as he had envisioned it. Certainly justification for a feeling of accomplishment.

No one could have foreseen the series of funny, pathetic, and exasperating contretemps that lay ahead!

The first notable event was the arrival of Bill. In November, the weather already growing cold, Bill appeared at the farm in a state of near-nudity. A night exposed to the elements would have put him in hospital. A glance from the police would have put him in jail. But he had managed somehow to find his way from the city.

One of the five residents tore off his own shirt and wrapped it around poor Bill and they took him to Annie. She was running the place; she would know what to do. They knew men were supposed to be referred by the "Provincial," but here was Bill admitting himself. Now that cold weather was settling in, men were heading to the farm directly from the streets, bypassing the hospital; Bill was just the first to arrive.

To everyone's surprise, Annie immediately took a shine to Bill. She took him into the Manor House, where she was living alone (the men were staying in the cottage) and took care of him herself. The next day she told the residents that Bill had the flu and was much too sick to work. Perhaps he had the flu (it would have been no great wonder) but there was no doubt in any of their minds that Bill was an alcoholic like themselves. That was why they were not pleased when, a week or so later, he appeared in slacks and a sports coat, white shirt and tie, and announced that he was the new farm manager and that, in future, any problems or questions should be brought to him.

Bill had landed on his feet. He had a good home—he lived in the Manor House with Annie; good food, and a good life—he had nothing to do with the other men, except to lord it over them. But nobody liked him—except Annie.

In the meantime, Dr. McLaughlin and Dr. Gregory were setting up a Board of Directors as required by the Government. Dr. Gregory sent the Department of Health a list of names of people who were interested in helping men with drinking problems, and a board was named. The president was an excellent choice, a respected businessman and philanthropist. But Dr. McLaughlin was not named. Lonewater's history was to be laced with such irony.

For example, the Manor House needed a new heating system, and the Province authorized a furnace and baseboard heating units. The bill came to $1,500. Annie paid it out of her own pocket. But Joe, the liaison man, took the receipt to Fredericton and claimed reimbursement. All well and good, except that Annie didn't see any of the money and a week or two later showed up at the same office with the same receipt. The Department paid again. Then, when the assets were listed for the farm's bill of sale, the heating system was included and the Province paid the third time! (According to the auditors, the furnace wasn't the only thing they paid for three times.)

In spite of stumbles, however, the Board and the Government carried on, and in due course the farm became Lonewater Foundation Inc., incorporated under the New Brunswick Companies Act. The Province then bought the farm and leased it back to the company for one dollar a year, and on the first of September, 1968, the company formally took control of the property.

On the seventh, I began my 18-year career as manager.

The qualifications for this position were two-fold. First, the manager must understand farming, for this was to be a working farm. Second, he must understand men; Lonewater was to be an important battleground in the community's fight against alcohol and drug abuse, and for the men who went there, a chance to wage personal battle against addiction. The right man for manager was essential.

I was invited by the Board to consider the post. Having recently retired from the Canadian Army, I was looking for another challenge, and a way to contribute to my home province now that I was back in New Brunswick. During my years in the army I had served in the United Kingdom, Italy and Northwest Europe during WW II, continued my service after the war and retired with the rank of Major. This put me in a position to lead men. During my service I held administrative positions and knew how to provide equipment, transport, and catering for small and large units of personnel either in camp or on manoeuvres. I was a country boy at heart, having grown up in Clifton Royal and Hampton, New Brunswick, son of a farming and lumbering family.

I accepted the challenge. My job description was vague, but a free hand was just what I wanted, and I was sure I could work with the Board to everyone's satisfaction. I could also work amicably with Dr. Ed Carten, my contact person at the Department of Health in Fredericton, who was not a medical man but a former teacher and superintendent of schools with a keen interest in the educational experiment we were undertaking at Lonewater.

My first priority was to ready the farm to receive up to 50 recovering alcoholics. My plan was to provide them with comfortable quarters, plenty of nourishing food, and outdoor exercise in abundance in the form of work on the land; meaningful work was to be part of their treatment. I should also provide wholesome recreation (both sports and indoor activities) as well as regular group discussions and individual counselling. I was to see that the centre ran smoothly and do my utmost to make it pay its own way. Other than that … (Well, no doubt problems would arise …) I was on my own!

The first problem that arose was the reaction of the community of Woodman's Point. This reaction has become known as the "Not-in-my-backyard Syndrome." Who wanted hordes of drunks in the neighbourhood? When I informed the residents of our problem with the neighbors, one of the Lonewater residents summed up the situation when he commented indignantly, "Just because we're alcoholics doesn't mean we're not gentlemen!"

I solved that problem by sending the men into the community to "help out." They kept roads open in winter and fought fires in summer. They did yard work for the elderly—

shovelled snow, cleaned garden spaces, and washed windows. They painted, repaired, built.... And some of them went to church on Sunday. Before long they made friends and were receiving visits and gifts in return.

Fortunately, under the Companies Act, Lonewater Farm could "solicit funds by way of gifts, donations, grants from the public and from governments of all levels ... also receive property at any time from any person, firm or corporation to be added to the capital assets of the Company provided such additional property [were] acceptable to the Company." In a word, "scrounge." I was in my element!

MY FIRST DAY ON THE JOB, I saw much that needed immediate attention. Except for the Manor House, which was a fine example of Loyalist construction, the buildings were not encouraging. All of them needed extensive repairs, and the old barn was tottering on its foundations, held up only by eight large decaying poles about twelve feet long braced against its west side.

The farm implements and machinery, except for a second-hand tractor Annie had bought after the Province took over, were also in a sad state of ruin, having been left out in rain and snow far too long. The farm vehicles as well (an old Dodge van and an old one-ton truck) had suffered years of neglect.

But the September woods were beginning to glow under the September sun, and Lonewater had roughly 900 acres of mature trees marching over the hills that rolled back from the river. That was a sight to cheer the heart of any country boy from New Brunswick. In my mind's eye I saw straight rows of pulpwood, cords of nice, dry firewood, logs to be turned into lumber.... And money in the bank. Besides, there were hay fields and gardens that could be productive and profitable. Lonewater might pay its way after all.

We had just finished lunch that first day. Bill and I were in Annie's study drawing up plans, when a head appeared around the door—Joe, the liaison man. "I brought groceries," he announced. "There'll be four or five more patients coming out from the Provincial tomorrow."

"You get out here and put away those groceries!" Annie shouted from the kitchen, and Joe disappeared.

"Good," I said to Bill. "I'll look forward to meeting these men."

"But, Major Flewwelling!" Bill bleated, "these guys are derelicts! Coming here is just keeping them out of jail."

"I disagree, Bill," I said firmly. "This farm is to be a place for chronic alcoholics to work while they learn to make a new life and take their rightful place in society. 'Sobriety through productivity' will be our motto."

Bill shook his head.

I continued, "I will not run a jail for any man. Here men will not serve time—time will serve them."

I could easily find space and work for the men expected on the following day. I thought back to the summer I ran a Militia Camp in New Brunswick (housing, feeding, transporting, and coordinating the training areas for 1,500 militia men and women) the first training camp ever run in Canada for soldiers of both sexes. In comparison, the farm would be fun.

Numbers grew steadily, from four or five in the beginning to eight, nine, eleven. Sixteen spent Christmas at the farm the first year, and they were only those who had nowhere to go or were afraid to face the temptations of the holiday season on their own.

I had soon worked out a routine for meeting new residents. They were welcomed with a firm handshake and friendly manner. At the same time I looked them straight in the eye and told them what I expected of them.

In time there were two sets of rules posted: the Fire Orders, which explained how to avoid causing fires and what to do if a fire broke out, and the Rules and Regulations.

First among the Rules and Regulations was, no alcohol on the premises. There would be no drinking on the Farm. Confiscated bottles would immediately become the property of the farm and would be poured down the sink by me, and there would be no smoking in bed.

As well, medicine of any kind, including over-the-counter drugs, was to be given to me and would be administered according to doctor's orders (a doctor visited twice a week.)

A man who broke these paramount rules would be sent away without plea or argument. But he might come back later, when he was ready to cooperate. My belief was that there are no hopeless situations, just men who have grown hopeless about them. Treat people as if they were what they ought to be and you help them to become what they are capable of being.

Whatever I said to a man, that man went away from the interview knowing that he had not heard a memorized lecture. Most alcoholics had heard their fill of homilies and recognized one coming from a long way off. What I gave them was straight talk from someone who cared, and they knew it.

From the beginning my aim was to operate the farm firmly but with kindness. The discipline of daily routine provided order; the staff, appointed from the residents, provided consideration and courtesy. Together these elements generated a tendency toward dignity, that had been missing in the lives of the residents all too long.

I encouraged the men to feel that they were participants in their rehabilitation. I might tell a man, "you are here because you want help. We will counsel you when you want to talk about your problems, but here we all work at something meaningful; that's an important part of your treatment. When you are assigned a task, you have already agreed with me that you are able and willing to perform that task, so I expect you to do it. If you don't do it (for any reason other than sickness) then don't show up at the table."

The residents were always informed of the various tasks that needed to be completed to keep the farm operational. "Here we don't order you to do a job; we ask you," was one of the sayings the men became used to hearing. Another was, "You don't work for me; you work with me, and I work with you."

There was no institutional "feel" at Lonewater. When the 1968 World Series began, for example, I adjusted the work schedule so that any man who was interested (and they were all ball fans!) could stop work and be in the lounge in good time for the games. Work, yes. Hard work, and lots of it. But also recovery. The ball games gave them a chance to relax and enjoy a common interest, which they appreciated the more because they had earned the privilege.

I chose a room on the ground floor of the Manor House for my office. French doors with oak shutters could be opened to provide plenty of air in warm weather, and there was a fireplace for warmth and cheer when the weather turned wet and cold. It was a pleasant room to work in.

The Manor House, like many grand houses of its period, faced the water. It was a fine, three-storey building showing skill and craftsmanship in every line and angle. All the wood in its construction had been hand-hewn from local timber, mainly pine and spruce. Nearly every room had a working fireplace, twelve in all. The house was then over 150 years old and had gone through periods of neglect, the worst a time of about twenty years when it was unoccupied except by vagrants and wood cutters, but it was still elegant.

Walking into the entrance hall was like walking into a church. Four large rooms opened from this spacious foyer: the dining room with a butler's pantry, two living rooms, and a study. It was the study that became my office.

The walls of the foyer were slightly curved to accommodate handsome mahogany doors that had been imported from England. They didn't look like mahogany when I arrived, for a previous owner had painted them a dark, flat green. But that was probably the reason they had survived; in their original state someone might have seen their value and stolen them.

A spiral staircase connected all three floors, leading down to the basement (not a cellar) where slave quarters and a kitchen had been located, and upstairs to the bedroom floor.

Two ells extended to the rear. Originally they had contained space for a wood house, an ice house, a dairy, and a coach house. One ell had a basement which at one time had contained a vegetable cellar and a wine cellar.

In this gracious setting, as 1968 drew to a close, I outlined a plan of that served me well for eighteen years. The details changed as I went along, but the structure remained the same. Everything in the plan worked toward the rehabilitation of the residents.

The men were organized into work crews. In the army, I

would have called these groups "platoons" or "troops," but I chose the word "crew" because I didn't want anyone to think I was running the farm on military lines with strict military discipline. I knew that the military life was not what these new soldiers needed. These were more like walking wounded, men not in hospital but not ready to fully care for themselves either.

A side view of the Manor House as it looked in 1970.

The plan I envisaged called for the establishment of a number of work programmes: woods work, field work, barn work, and so on. Each resident would choose the programme that seemed right for him. If there seemed to be no programme that was right for any particular man, then he would be assigned to general upkeep of the buildings: cleaning the houses, helping in the kitchen, doing grounds work, until something turned up that required the skills and interests he already possessed. I aimed to make Lonewater Farm as self-sufficient as possible by matching residents' talents to the Farm's requirements. This required patience. If, for instance, we needed an electrician we might have to wait a long time for one to arrive.

Each programme was carried on by a crew or crews. My chart listed Kitchen Crew, Wood Crew, Maintenance Crew, Barn Crew, Farm Crew, and Hut Crew. The most skilled or experienced member of each crew was appointed foreman. And as the farm filled with men and the crews fleshed out, positions of storeman and farm foreman were added.

The first farm foreman was Elton Langille from St.

Martins. Langille was a big man with wavy grey hair. He had been a farm boy who had worked in the woods from a young age, and he had been an army sergeant. He was strong as an oak. Except for his problem with alcohol he was disciplined. And he was a hard worker.

Langille arrived at the farm with the group that came on my second day at Lonewater Farm. I soon saw his potential, and besides becoming my right hand in matters of farming and logging, Langille would be my ally in the fight to keep alcohol off the premises. He would be close enough to the men that they would confide in him, but he would have no compunction in telling me if any of them started drinking. I had to know as soon as possible, and from my days in the military I knew it was often hard to tell if a man was drinking, especially if he did so regularly. Elton Langille was invaluable to me and we became lifelong friends.

At first the duties of the farm foreman could be summed up in the phrase "the Major's right hand man." Eventually, when the Alcoholism and Drug Dependency Commission of New Brunswick took over from Lonewater Inc., he became responsible for the maintenance of all equipment used for farming, maintenance of the field and garden areas to a high standard for the best yield, maintenance of stored vegetables to a grade that could be used by the kitchen, maintenance of the farm roadways; also for running the wood-cutting operations and for ensuring that all the residents were employed on a schedule of duties that rotated week by week.

To say that Elton Langille was capable of accomplishing all these tasks when I first appointed him farm foreman would be stretching the truth, but he had the potential. Besides the skills and attitudes necessary to run a large farm, he had an intimate, habitual, intuitive familiarity with the land, the crops, and the weather. And he had that quality required of all leaders: every man and every animal on the farm recognized him as foreman. Elton Langille had presence.

The army of walking wounded was shaping up.

CHAPTER TWO

The Search

AUTHOR'S NOTE:
James Mason wrote a quasi-fictional account of the often long and painful road men travelled to sanctuary, help, and recovery at Lonewater Farm. This chapter is based on that account.

HE WOKE TO MUFFLED SOUNDS OF TRAFFIC, but he was unsure where the sounds were coming from. Some place ... out there.

He made an effort to raise himself from the ground, but gave it up. Finding out where he was could come later. Now he preferred to find out why he was there. Except that he knew why already. Because he was a drunk. A damned drunk. That much he knew.

The other why—why he had gotten drunk this time—he worked on to take his mind off the first. "Because of Lisa," he thought. "An ex-wife's phone call will do that to you—especially when she tells you she's married again."

He lay on the ground and thought about Lisa's voice. Her tone had conveyed ... relief. Relief! The word echoed in his mind. That was why he had started this time.

He focused on the scene in front of him. Cars rushed by. The noises were hitting him harder now. Individual jabs of pain pricked his head. He was lying beside the approach to the Reversing Falls Bridge, the railway bridge, but he couldn't remember how he got there.

"It must be Saturday morning," he thought. "Quite warm for September. But it'll rain later." He didn't know how he knew these things.

He turned away from the bridge and picked his way along

the tracks. Suppose he fell on the rails and lay there all night....

"Keep moving," he told himself.

Coming to a dirt path that intersected the railroad, he saw a crabapple tree and stopped to examine its speckling of tiny red fruit. The really good ones were higher up the tree.

"Of course," he said aloud.

Several apples lay on the ground within easy reach, and he picked one up.

Eating the apple sharpened his need for food. He reached for his wallet to make sure he had money, and that was the last he remembered. For some time afterward he lay on the ground.

"You okay there?"

Someone had spoken to him, was helping him up.

He wanted to say he was fine, but he couldn't get the words out—the man's face stopped him cold. He had seen that look on other faces—a grimace of disgust, loathing.

The man walked away slowly, not looking back. He accepted that. Tried to ignore it, forget it.

Glancing down at himself he saw what that man had seen. He was dishevelled, dirty. A figure in need of help. More than ordinary help. Tears came to his eyes and overflowed. He felt the sting of them.

The thought came to return to his room on Douglas Avenue. It was only a short walk from where he was.

He no longer felt hunger, but thirst. Water thirst.

"That's what I'll do," he muttered. "Go back to the house. Clean up. Get a drink of water."

The woman who collected the rent must have seen him coming; she was waiting for him by the door.

Before he said anything she pointed to a suitcase in the corner of the hall. "If you hadn't come back for your things, I was going to call your ex," she said. "I thought you were picking that up last night."

Last night?

He couldn't remember anything about picking up his things.

The woman understood. "Look, Mike, why don't you take Gary's advice and go to the farm like he said you should? It sure did him a world of good!"

"Is Gary in now?" he asked.

"No, but he left you this," she said, and reached into her pocket for an envelope with his name on it.

He tore open the envelope. Before he could read the note he saw the $10 bill that had been placed in front of it. He put the money in his wallet. Then he unfolded the note. There were only a few words: *Mike, take the money. Go to the farm.*

"Make the decision," he thought. "Make it. What have you got to lose?"

He walked out of the yard to the street and kept walking, heading west, heading upriver, heading for Lonewater Farm.

Once the decision was made, his strength began to return. He would need it. The distance he had to cover was 16 miles.

He didn't try to hitch a ride from passing cars. People wouldn't pick up anyone like him. Dirty. Needing a shave. Mouth hanging open with fatigue.

So he walked, mile after mile, till he could walk no longer and sank down at the side of the road.

His mind had begun to wander when a truck pulled up beside him and a man called from the window.

"You need a lift there, friend?"

Mike made a half-hearted effort to stand but was unsuccessful. Oddly enough, he wanted to laugh.

"Just a minute," he heard.

The man who had stopped for him was a big, burly fellow. He steadied him as he helped him to his feet with no more effort, it seemed, than he would have used to pick up a baby. Maybe that was a good sign. It might be nice to be a baby, starting out, starting over.

"Heading for Lonewater, are you?" the man asked. "I'm going in that direction."

Mike got into the truck.

After a few miles the truck stopped where a side road met the main highway. "You just start down that road," the big man said. "You don't have far to go now. Okay?"

Mike turned and spoke to the man for the first time. "I appreciate the lift," he said. "I'll be all right from here."

The man smiled and raised his right hand as if in

benediction. “Take care,” he said.

He would. He was already taking care. He was on the right road.

“I came here for ...” he stammered to the first person he met at the farm. “I mean, I was told ... to come here. By a friend. He said they take people ...”

“We do take ‘em,” the stranger said. “Look, you come with me. We’ll get you straightened away in no time.”

Mike followed his guide to a big old house and then into a large room where a fire glowed in an open fireplace and a man sat working at an antique mahogany desk.

Momentarily Mike wondered if he had come to the right place, but the man behind the desk rose and extended his hand.

“I’m Major Flewwelling,” he said. “We’re glad to have you here. Take a seat.”

The Major believed every man deserved a second chance, more if necessary.

The Major indicated a chair beside his desk, and Mike sank into it, releasing his grip on his suitcase for the first time.

“Now, you have to have medical clearance before you can stay here,” the Major explained. “We can arrange that at the Ridgewood Treatment and Rehabilitation Centre. Someone will drive you there. It won’t take long. But first you look like you could use something to eat.”

As Mike drew a deep breath, he glanced through the French

doors to the sunporch. Rain was spattering the windows.

"I got here in time," he said. "I got here just in time."

"TIME TO GO, MIKE."

The voice of his roommate was not loud but it was firm. "We'll head down to the dining room for breakfast."

Mike stood up from his seat on the edge of his bed. He was feeling not too bad. The Ridgewood doctor had told him he was in reasonably good shape for someone in his condition. It was a relief to know he hadn't destroyed his health altogether … yet.

"A stay at the farm is just what you need at this point," the doctor had said. "A couple of months working there will help you get straightened around."

Well, at least he was hungry.

"Food's all right, eh?"

This question came from a little fellow sitting across the table, who appeared to be enjoying his breakfast even more than Mike was enjoying his.

"I work in the barn," the little man said with pride. "I'm responsible for some of the stuff you're eating. Well, me and some other fellows. Now you take them eggs—we got hens right here. And cows. Never milked a cow in my life till I came here. Now there's a story …."

Mike smiled but kept eating. He was going to be working in the woods and he didn't want to be hungry later on. He had chosen the woods crew because he had always liked being out in the open, being in the woods. As a boy he had lived in a rural area. A short walk and he could be away from houses and cars and into the peace he found among the trees.

"So now I'm back, at least for the time being," he thought.

A loud, friendly voice spoke from the doorway. "Okay, boys. Let's get going. The day's not getting any younger and neither are we. Let's get a move on."

Mike looked up at a big, muscular man who winked at him.

"That's Elton Langille, the Duke," the talkative one across the table said. "He's farm foreman. Directly under the Major. You'll like him. Everybody does. He'll look after you. Used to work in the woods at one time. Knows what he's doing, Duke does."

"You should have been here in old Annie's day," the man beside him murmured. "They say the Duke liked to tease her something awful. When she came around he'd give her a big squeeze and tell her what a fine figure of a woman she was. And she'd laugh.... Never saw old Annie myself, but they say she had a face that'd stop a clock."

The Duke walked over to Mike and put a hand on his shoulder. "You're with us today, are you?" he said, and Mike felt like one of the team already.

A woods crew — fresh air and hard work were welcome medicine for some residents.

"I can see why they made him foreman," he thought.

By lunchtime he had decided that cutting pulp and hardwood wasn't bad. His job was to pile up limbs and bits of brush left by the men who used the chain saws. Nobody used the saws who wasn't accustomed to them—too dangerous, but he was already thinking he might like to learn. It looked like fun, and he could see that nobody was pushed beyond his strength. Up to his strength, maybe, but not beyond it. The idea was clearly to build the men up physically, not to wear them out—or to make money from them.

When lunch arrived from the kitchen, they all dropped their tools and relaxed on the piles of trees they had cut, eating hearty sandwiches and drinking tea they had brewed on a small fire.

"How long you planning to stay?" somebody asked Mike.

"I don't know," he replied. "I mean, I don't know how long I'll need ... how long it'll take...."

Part of the recovery was to know others struggled with the same demons, and won.

"Sure. Some guys are here a week," one man told him. "Then it's back to the city. That's all they needed, you know. Just a short stay."

"Yeah, but not everybody learns the first time," somebody else chimed in. "Me, I guess I'm a hard case. I been here a long time. I've seen men come back here more than once. But at the same time I've seen them go out after just one stay and never come back. Some get turned around and even back with their families, no problem. There was that fellow came to visit just the other day ..."

He appealed to the others.

"One with the good looking wife?" a young man asked with a grin.

"That's him. She's a looker, ain't she? Him and me came

here first together, but he's been fine now two or three years."

"We had a bunch of university students one day not long ago," the Duke said. "Touring the farm like they do every year. Part of their course or something. They were some pretty, too. We kept them as long as we could."

"We had a visit from a church group one time, too," another man said. "The Major invited them after they gave us a gas stove they weren't using any more."

"Count on the Major to go scrounging," somebody else said with a laugh.

"A fellow even came down from Ontario once," the Duke told him. "Just to see how this place works. He was impressed, too. They don't have many places like this anywhere else, so the Major says."

In the evening, after they had finished dinner, Mike was free to choose what he would do. He looked around at the others. Some went to the recreation hall to watch television or to play cards, or pool, or just to talk. Others gathered for an Alcoholics Anonymous meeting.

Mike sat in for awhile at a party for a fellow called Eddy who just turned 39—so he said! They had brought a birthday cake to the table and Eddy was passing out slices of that and telling stories on himself. When he beckoned Mike to join him and his friends, he was telling about the time he had this beautiful girlfriend, only she was blind as a bat, almost. Eddy himself wore glasses so thick they looked like a pair of alarm clocks, but—according to him—the girl was even worse. She never wore glasses, though. Funny thing, but she never did. Well, sir, one day Eddy is a few dollars ahead, so he takes the girlfriend uptown and buys her a nice, new pair of spectacles.

You guessed it! She takes one look at Eddy, and he hasn't seen her since!

After Eddy's party Mike went over to the Peters' house where there was a hobby-crafts area. Some of the men made miniature fireplaces for sale in the city. Others made things like puzzles or little leather ornaments with Saint John's Loyalist-Man symbol on them. The really good workers made leather wallets and ladies purses. He had seen some of those things displayed in a case in the foyer of the Manor House.

As he was standing by one of the work tables watching a fellow lace a wallet, a man entered the building to a chorus of "Hi, Relic," and seeing a newcomer, he walked up and stuck out his hand.

"I'm the fellah that does the instructing," he said. "You interested in crafts?"

"I've done some wood work," Mike answered.

Some work from the hobby shop.

"Then you want the carpentry shop," Relic told him. "I'm on my way over there. Come along if you like."

Mike could smell the wood in his head. He'd like that.

"We once made a stand for the New Brunswick Museum in the city," Relic told him as they walked between buildings. "They had a big ship's wheel there, and they wanted a stand for it so they could show people how the steering worked on the old sailing ships. Kids love it because it actually works. I mean, it's connected to a chain so they can move it and hear the chain rattle and feel the weight just like they were really on an old ship."

Mike knew where he would be hanging out in his spare time.

"I'll be back," he said to Relic as he left the shop.

"Good," Relic said. "We can use another pair of hands with Christmas coming."

One more stop, for a snack before going to bed, and Mike met a friendly, talkative fellow who introduced himself as editor of the farm newspaper, *The Hitching Post*.

"I put out *The Post* once a week," he said. "It keeps the boys informed as to what's happening here at the farm and elsewhere

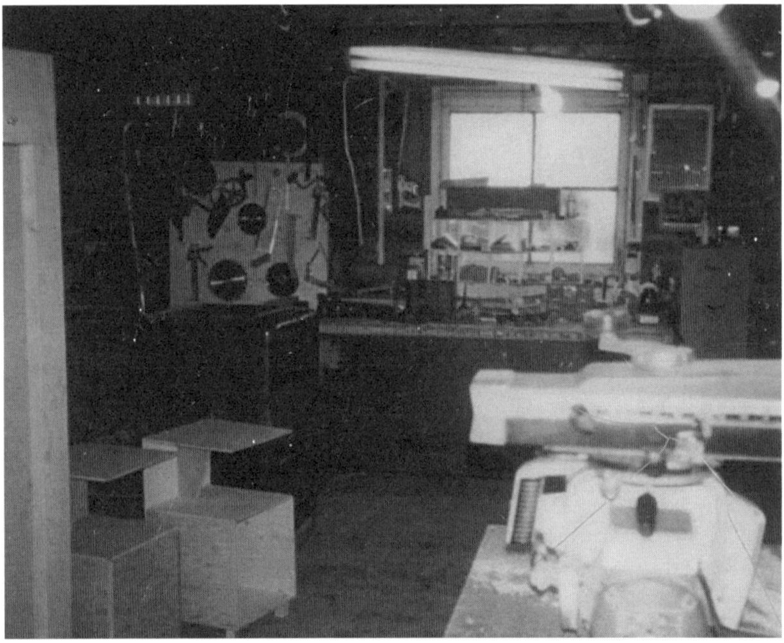

Some nice work came out of the carpentry shop.

in the province. We mention matters such as government policy on alcoholism and rehabilitation in New Brunswick. We also try to include information on ex-residents. Some of them are doing all right. About 120 men have come through here in the past year, so there's never a shortage of copy, but if you ever have anything that you want to give us, just let me know. I work evenings using the typewriter in the office at the Manor House."

"I'll do that," Mike said.

Back in his room, his roommate clapped him on the shoulder and asked him if his arms and legs were still working after his first day in the woods.

“Well, I hope you’ll like it here,” he said. “Some guys complain about being so far from town, but we get to go to things sometimes—wrestling, hockey games, stuff like that.”

“Yes, I know,” Mike said, “I have to go to town next Friday.”

“Well, just be sure you’re on Hazen Avenue by 4:30 if you want a ride back. You better be sober, too. Guys get turned away for having a pint in them.”

“That’s not going to happen to me,” Mike said. “I’ve got a chance here. I’m not going to blow it.”

CHAPTER THREE

Lonewater Begins to Feel Established

UNTIL THE MID-SEVENTIES, I RAN LONEWATER Farm with little input from the Province, except financial help and the encouragement and advice of Dr. Carten. Most years the farm paid its own way. The farm foreman worked with me. While Bill stayed, he continued in the office as bookkeeper; afterward, some other resident was always able to take over that work. The other men did everything else: crops, animals, logging, building, maintenance—everything required to make the farm a home and a success, both functionally and financially.

The men counselled each other, the stronger or better educated helping the weaker. Professional counsellors were often horrified by this system when I informed them how we operated at the Farm but the participants thought it worked very well. Some resident counsellors confessed they had sometimes told the ones they counselled things that they should have practised themselves. As Dr. Carten understood very well, they were using sound teaching practice.

For the rest, Lonewater made many friends. Dr. Sean Keyes visited regularly from Saint John and charged no fees. (Two other doctors, Dr. Moar and Dr. McLaughlin, took over when Dr. Keyes had done more than his share.) Members of Alcoholics Anonymous came to hold regular and frequent meetings. I would invite members of church and service clubs to a meal with the men and usually they went away planning what they could do to help. Two very socially prominent ladies often came out to help price the hand bags, wallets, belts, and other items the residents made in the hobby shop. One of those ladies showed the barn crew how to use a turnip slicer; she had used one as a girl growing up on a farm. She turned the handle so hard that the slices of the turnip went halfway across the barn.

Everyone who experienced those first years says that they were good years, and some say that they were the best of all.

ONE OF THE EARLY IMPROVEMENTS I undertook on the farm was to gather all the machinery and equipment into one place. Much of it had been left out in the elements and was in bad shape. The men spent two or three days finding things and hauling them to the old, pole-construction wagon shed across from the barn. For this job they used the tractor that Annie had bought.

After the equipment was assembled, the shed had to be reinforced and extended. The crew cut a few small logs for rafters and frame, then gathered up old boards that lay here and there about the place, which they used for the roof, sides, and end of the shed—the front was open, facing south. They used old corrugated iron for the roof.

The wagon shed was a success. Everyone enjoyed the work and the accomplishment. It looked pretty good, too.

When the wagon shed was finished, I set the men to propping up the barn. That meant new posts under the structure and long poles to buttress the west side, which had a lean of about 24 degrees. Finding, cutting, preparing, and placing thick posts and 16-foot poles occupied another couple of weeks.

Again the men enjoyed the work and the accomplishment, and it was satisfying to know that the barn was secure, at least for the winter. After all, a dozen or more hens and three cows (one on loan from a friend of the farm who hadn't a barn of his own at the time) lived in that building; and the barn crew worked there. Safety was important.

Also important were the eggs and milk, if the farm were to be self-sufficient. The hens were supplying almost enough eggs for the needs of the kitchen, and the cows more than enough milk. Surplus milk was separated for cream. The $90 or so a month that they earned from the sale of cream was the first income they produced, and might have been gold nuggets.

Looking back over the years from the vantage point of the new barn the men built and of the new wagon shed they put up when the old one burned, it may seem that these first accomplishments were pretty insignificant, but it is not likely that the later residents derived any more satisfaction from their successes than those early workers did from theirs.

Farm life gave the men a sense of pride in themselves.

BY CHRISTMAS TIME, Lonewater Farm was beginning to feel established. Sixteen men stayed for the holidays. All had hard Christmas memories to look back on (some Christmases had disappeared from memory altogether) and I wanted Christmas, 1968, to be their best in a long time.

To that end I went on the scrounge, calling every company that had done business with the farm and asking for donations. The grocery stores contributed. So did the hardware stores and department stores.

The Duke and Relic (so named because he reminded everyone of Relic of the popular CBC TV series) went into the woods and cut a tree which they set up in one of the large living rooms of the Manor House. It brushed the ceiling at 12 feet. Annie supplied lights and trimmings that she had on hand, I bought more, and the tree was a sight to behold. Some of the men tied greenery to fasten above the doorways in the hall and in the other houses. The farm had not been so festive for years.

On Christmas morning the residents woke to find that each had received a bag filled with presents. There were socks, cigarettes, candy, apples and oranges, razors, gloves, handkerchiefs, soap and combs, a flashlight and a jackknife for everyone, and a small box of cigars.

Later the Duke cooked a turkey dinner with all the trimmings, including mince pie.

"YOU will cook Christmas dinner?" I had asked.

"Of course," The Duke replied. "Used to cook in the woods when I was no more than so high."

A man of many talents.

Christmas week festivities ended with a visit and concert by some of the Sisters of Charity from Saint John. Annie was delighted when she heard the Sisters were coming and organized a big lunch in honour of the occasion. Everybody enjoyed the evening. The men had spent a few days relaxing, and the concert was the perfect way to top off their break.

The Sisters began by singing some songs they had composed themselves and closed with a round of Christmas carols, which the men sang with them. They were accompanied by a very good guitarist, and long afterward the farm remembered the Sisters and their "mean guitar."

So a momentous few months drew to a close, and some of the funny, pathetic, and exasperating incidents (sometimes all three at once) that nobody could have foreseen were already history.

Christmas Day had been fine and had brought many visitors to the farm, one of them a particular friend who some time before had asked me, "How many men will you have over Christmas?"

"Sixteen," I replied.

The first Christmas tree brushed the ceiling at 12 feet.

"Buy them all overshoes and send me the bill," he said.

On Christmas Day the friend came to visit. He hung up his coat, put his hat and gloves on a shelf above the coat rack, and joined the men to see how they were spending the holiday. When he left, he put on his coat, took his hat in his hand, and reached up for his gloves. Puzzled, he turned to me.

"My gloves are gone!" he exclaimed.

"Oh, they must be there," I said.

"No. Someone has taken my new Christmas gloves!"

I was taken aback, unwilling to believe that any of the residents had taken them. Other visitors had placed identical gloves on that rack. Maybe his had been taken by mistake.

"I doubt it, Major," the friend said, shaking his head.

He turned up his collar and walked out into the snow-packed driveway.

"Anyway, it's good for me," he muttered.

"Good for you?"

"Of course. Serves me right. Patting myself on the back for my overwhelming generosity. Sixteen pairs of overshoes! It's the law of the self-righteous, Major: no good deed shall go unpunished."

Just after Christmas the weather turned cold, very cold, and the sewer line from the Manor House to the septic tank stopped working. Was it frozen, or was there another reason?

I asked Annie to show me where the septic tank was located,

but she had no idea. This could be a problem! But Duke and I trooped down to the basement and traced the sewer pipe to locate the direction it took when it left the house. Then some of the men went out in the bitter cold and dug three or four holes, without success. The ground was very hard, the wind very cold, and I called a halt to the operation.

The next day I borrowed from the City an instrument they used to find water lines. The Duke and I found the direction, and a crew of volunteers drove three indicator stakes into the ground. That was enough work in the cold for another day.

The following morning I hired a backhoe, and a section of the ground was dug down to the pipe. Then two residents, wearing rubber boots and armed with a wire snake, cleared the line. It was plugged with plastic bags. A new resident had a colostomy, and nobody had thought to warn him. Oh, well … I hired a plumber to repair the pipe, the residents filled in the hole, and Bill printed up neat notices: Residents will please refrain from … etc.

DURING THE EARLY PART OF THE YEAR heavy snow fell on southern New Brunswick and reduced the work around the farm to a minimum. To keep the men busy I introduced new plans: to create the position of storeman, to set one man in charge of the mechanics' shop, and to set up a properly constituted barn crew.

We cleared out one ell of the Manor House to establish an area for the storeman. Removing all the useless items stored there and carting them to the dump kept five men busy for several days.

When the ell was clear, we discovered a cellar under it that the first owners had used for cold storage. It was cleverly designed so that large cakes of ice from the ice house could be slid into two boxes without having to be lifted. In those days during the winter, people along the river cut ice in large blocks and stored them in sawdust (which helped prevent thawing) till they should be needed during the summer.

With the new storeroom ready, and a man in charge of keeping a record of all items in store, used, or needed, I turned their

This small shed was turned into a garage.

attention to a small shed which they cleared out for mechanical work. They even found a stove among the assets, which they set up for heat. Once the work of cutting wood began, the Duke used the mechanics' shed for sharpening the chain saws.

At the same time I placed a new resident, a man who had grown up on a farm, in charge of the barn. He was called "Barney," naturally.

Barney got the job because he knew what he was talking about when he spoke about farming.

When he first arrived, the hens were not laying well, in spite of enjoying the best of poultry rations. Barney suggested that they be placed in a dark room to moult for a while. Sure enough, in a week or two the hens were back and laying again.

One day Barney reported that a rat had killed a hen. He could tell by the bite on the hen's neck, he said, that the culprit was a rat. I wasn't convinced of the rat theory, but a few days later Barney reported another dead hen and again insisted that the blame should be laid at the door of some rat. Four hens died in this way.

"Perhaps it's a weasel," I suggested.

"No," Barney said. "It's a rat."

Again I shook my head.

After that Barney kept careful watch, and a few mornings later came galloping into my office with a big grin on his face. Proof. He had seen two rats eating out of the hens' trough, along with the hens.

Rats, Barney figured, must be pretty smart. At least the ones at Lonewater were. In his opinion it took a good deal of intelligence to figure out that hens meant hen-food and absence of hens would mean absence of hen-food—hence, a truce: the rats would not kill any more hens if the hens would share their table.

Nobody was ever able to prove Barney wrong, and no more hens died.

About this time, too, both a plumber and a carpenter arrived at the farm as residents, and I was able to set up a maintenance crew. These men and their helpers were kept very busy. They made a bedside table for every man in residence, mended doors and windows, repaired taps and toilets.

Along with the hut crew, who kept the houses clean, and a kitchen crew, who did the cooking, the list was now complete. Every man was well occupied at meaningful work.

Clothing for the men was always in short supply that first winter. Most of them had arrived very ill-equipped and had no means to provide for themselves.

I called on all the funeral homes, church organizations, and other groups or businesses that wouldn't require payment, but I never scrounged enough. When the weather grew very cold in February, I made a deal with the owner of a war surplus store: battle dress pants and tunics, gloves, socks, and boots in exchange for a little money and the promise of a load of hardwood stove-lengths. Problem solved.

My plan for Lonewater was working well, and the press soon learned about it. One day a reporter showed up with a camera. His very favourable story referred to "the Major's private army that marched to a different drum" and was the first of many references and a few feature articles. Lonewater might be marching to a different drum, but it was definitely forging ahead.

During this time, however, Annie became a problem. She was still living in the Manor House, taking up a big bedroom and one of the main living rooms, which was crammed with her furniture. As well, she was keeping control of the kitchenette and the dining room.

"I'm not doing any harm here," she argued. "What's wrong with taking up one little room in this great big house? Nobody ever notices me."

Unfortunately, I noticed her—all the time. If I had a man in my office for counselling, or for any other reason, Annie would march in and put in her five cents worth.

"I wish I'd been born a man," she would growl. "I'd soon make you fellows work."

Furthermore when I had a room arranged to my liking, she would rearrange it.

I knew, as well, that she wasn't always truthful with me. One morning, Bill confessed that he hadn't come to the farm as a resident at all, that Annie had gone to Fredericton to hire him to manage the office. Annie corroborated that story. She said a friend had told her about Bill.

In December, at a Board meeting, I had suggested that Annie might be asked to leave, now that she no longer owned the property.

"No, no," they said. "She's not doing any harm. Just let nature take its course. The situation will resolve itself."

But I couldn't make Annie understand that she was no longer running the farm; that, in fact, she shouldn't even be there, having agreed with the government when they bought the place that she would leave in September. It was now the middle of February.

Since it was clear that the Board wasn't going to ask Annie to leave, I took matters into my own hands. I explained to her that we could put three men in her big bedroom and that we needed the second living room to set up a rainy day programme, such as a hobby shop. I told her, moreover, that as she had a nice little cottage at Woodman's Point I would have the men help her move.

At first Annie was angry and raved on about injustices, but in the end she blamed the government, not me.

Once she realized that leaving was inevitable, she began to

bargain. She said that she had an apartment in Halifax that she had to vacate and it would be convenient to her to borrow the truck and three men to help her move. "What could I do to help her?" Here was a chance to rid myself of an aggravation. I agreed that if she would take financial responsibility, the Farm would assist her. Two days later Annie was ready to go, with three men in the truck and Bill to drive her car.

I saw them off and breathed more freely at once, but Annie's move from Halifax was not without a lesson in the vagaries of alcoholism: that any excuse is justification for a binge. Two days later Annie and Bill came back without the three men in the truck. They were discovered pulled off the road near Truro trying to sober up.

They told me that after a day carrying furniture down three flights of stairs and loading the truck they were tired. Of course they were. But Annie started right back. About midnight, however, feeling tired herself, she stopped the truck and told the men they should find a place to sleep. They thought she meant she was going to put them up at a motel, but she meant they should find a place to pull off the road and sleep as best they could. Of course they were disgusted, but their reaction was self-destructive. They found a place to buy a bottle first; then they found a place to spend the night.

I was always saddened when the men slipped back into their old ways, but they were under my care, not incarcerated, and I had to let them try their resolve from time to time.

More than once I had to take a bottle away from one of the men and deal with the situation immediately. The punishment was instant expulsion, but sometimes, if there were extenuating circumstances, the offender might be allowed to stay. The design at Lonewater was to reform men, not to destroy them. The Duke once caught a resident with a bottle under his bed and asked me to go easy on him. He gave two reasons: the bottle had been smuggled in by a visitor, and the man was a good worker. Being a good worker counted for a lot on the Farm.

At first this resident was prepared to fight to keep his bottle.

"All right, which would you rather have," I asked him, "a

bed and plenty of good food, or a bottle and nowhere to live?" That was the end of the struggle.

Another resident brought a bottle back from the city and refused to hand it over. When he threatened to fight, I took my coat off and said, "Okay, the best man gets the bottle." End of problem.

Sometimes, though, we had to call the police. An ex-resident returned to the farm very drunk and insisted that he was going to stay. When the RCMP arrived, he took one look at the young female officer behind the wheel of the car and swore that he wasn't going to be hauled away by anyone, least of all a woman.

The officer got out of the car, drew her gun, and stood with her back against a wall. "It's your choice," she said. "You can leave in my car, or you can leave in the ambulance." The man got into the car. That was probably the only time a weapon was needed to control a situation at the farm.

I had to call the police from time to time, of course, but not often. On one occasion I was staying at the farm overnight instead of returning to my home as I usually did. I called them, because just as I was settling down for the night, I received a phone call from a neighbour saying that two drunks were stumbling along Campbell Road toward the farm gate.

I knew that these two were not residents, as our men were all in bed at the time. To be a good neighbour, however, I drove to where the men had been seen, and found them in bad shape. They were heading for Lonewater Farm, they said.

"You can't get into the farm when you have been drinking," I told them. "Go back to wherever you came from."

While I waited for the police, I strolled out to the gate with a powerful flashlight. I didn't turn the light on, just held it ready.

In a few minutes I heard the crunch of footsteps on gravel. They were coming into the lane. Just as the first one came abreast of me, I switched on the light and demanded in a loud voice, "Where do you think you're going?"

The man leapt into the air and came down sober. "My God!" he hollered. "You almost scared me to death!"

The two seemed harmless, and for the sake of the neighbourhood I let them stay overnight and sober up.

When they were settled, I rang the police to cancel my earlier call, but no officer had been sent; they hadn't anyone available. That fact spoiled the enjoyment of my midnight adventure. The farm was obviously in a vulnerable position, if anyone ever wanted to make serious trouble.

CHAPTER FOUR

We Start to Cut Wood

ONE MORNING EARLY IN JANUARY THE Duke stood in my office looking out across the barnyard. We were discussing the work for the day and I was lecturing on the need to cut down waste in the barn.

"Look!" Duke exclaimed. "It's a quarter to three!"

"A quarter to three!" I looked at my watch. "What are you talking about? It's only half past eight in the morning!"

"Come and see!" Duke said.

Coming toward us from across the yard was a new man, scuttling along with his toes turned out like the hands of a clock. The new man already had his farm name. And although the foreman couldn't know it at the time, he was about to earn his.

MY SUMMARY OF ACTIVITIES for the year 1969 shows that Item One was to start the wood operation, which was to be the first big income-maker.

Just after the new year began, Dr. Carten dropped in for a visit in his official capacity as Director of Alcoholic Programmes for the New Brunswick Department of Health.

After a walk around to show him the work that had already been done, I took Dr. Carten to the office to review my plans for cutting pulp, logs and firewood. He now had two men well qualified to operate chain saws, having spent a great deal of their working lives in the woods. One was the farm foreman; the other was a chap called John. Several others were fit and willing to act as helpers.

My plan was to have three men to a crew, one to cut and the others to pile and help as required. The man with the saw would be foreman. To outfit two crews we needed two new chain saws. We already had one, but we would need that as backup. We also needed safety equipment: hard hats, steel-toed boots, knee pads ... and a horse and harness.

Dr. Carten raised his eyebrows at the horse. "I thought you had a tractor," he said.

"Oh, yes," I replied. "We have a tractor. But we're going into the woods in winter. There will be places in there where a tractor would stall and become useless, even dangerous, especially on steep slopes. We'll need a horse."

Dr. Carten raised one eyebrow. "Like horses, do you?" he remarked.

"Yes, I really do."

"All right," Dr. Carten agreed. "You know what you're doing. I'll approve the bills."

"I'll keep my eyes open for a suitable animal," I said.

At this time, the farm had a Board of Directors, but there was really very little for them to do. They had no expertise in the field of rehabilitation, and the Department of Health was paying the bills. The Board was required by the Companies Act to meet annually; that was all. They met perhaps quarterly. Dr. Carten and I were, therefore, free to make such decisions without prior permission from the Board.

In a few days I had purchased the equipment and organized the crews. That done, I took the Duke and we cruised the woodlot nearest the farm. Since I had grown up in a lumbering family and knew something about cutting pulp, I soon realized that my farm foreman was an experienced woodsman and did not hesitate to put him in full charge.

Having selected the leader, the area to be harvested, and the size of trees to be cut (they were to practise selective harvesting) I called the six men to my office and explained how their operation was to work.

Cutters were to be paid $3.00 a cord; helpers $1.50. I pointed out that if they were working for a contractor they would be required to supply everything they were getting free at the farm: equipment, room and board, the lot. In that way, I explained, the low wages worked out to be fair.

Since there was little snow at that time, the logs would be hauled out using the tractor and piled near the barn. Tractor driver and helper would also be paid $1.50 a cord each.

The men went into the woods keen to start, but after only a few days John and his crew trooped into my office in the middle of the afternoon and formed a semi-circle in front of my desk.

"Major," John said, "I think we're through here. We don't feel we're getting a fair shake. I mean, we should be getting more for our work. We don't mind staying, but we'll have to be paid the going rate or we'll go where they'll pay us what we're worth."

I paused to gather my thoughts. I understood that these men were worth the wages paid by the industry, but they were at Lonewater for rehabilitation, not for regular employment.

"I understand your concerns," I said. "However, this logging operation costs money to run. We sent the Department of Health a number of large bills for equipment just this week. If they weren't footing the bill, we wouldn't be logging at all. We also have the fixed costs of running and maintaining the truck and the tractor, as well as the chain saws. Then we have to pay your costs and your wages, in addition to your room and board.

Nobody spoke.

"Lonewater Farm costs a lot to run," I went on. "Although it is supported by the Department of Health, it must pay its own way as far as possible; so if the logging operation is to be part of our success, it must be run on sound business lines. Now, the cost of supporting a resident is figured into the wages you are all paid, regardless of the kind of work you do. This is the only way the farm can become self-sufficient....

I looked at each man in turn.

"The farm is going to be self-sufficient," I said. "And that, gentlemen, is something to be proud of."

The two helpers studied the floor.

"Besides," I finished, "the reason you are working in the woods is that it is part of your rehabilitation program."

"I'm sorry, Major," John replied, "but I know we can make more elsewhere, even paying for our own equipment and living costs. If you won't pay us what we're worth, we'll go where we can get fair wages."

John was not to be moved. He had made up his mind, and he was certain he had made the right decision.

I didn't want to lose this skilled worker. Nor did I want to lose him to his old way of life. But I had to stand for what I knew was right for the farm, for the men, and for the continuity of the programme. Lonewater wouldn't last till the end of the month if I caved in every time someone disagreed with me.

"If that is how you feel, John," I said, "then perhaps you had better leave. I'll take you to Saint John."

I rose and looked at the others. "Each of you must make your own decision," I told them. "You can go back to work, or you can leave with John."

They were quiet a moment. Then they stepped back, stammering their wish to stay on the farm.

Relieved that I hadn't destroyed the woods operation altogether, I nodded. "Best get back to work, then."

Then I turned to John. "Be ready at the door of the Manor House in twenty minutes," I told him.

On the way to the city I told John that any time he felt that he could take our programme, we would be happy to have him back. As the days passed, I worried about him. I knew my own decision was the only one I could have made, but I wondered if John was all right and if he would have the guts to come back if he needed help.

After a week or so I was working at his desk when there was a loud knock at the door. "Major!"

It was John.

"Major, I'm ready to go back to work," he said.

"Well, that's fine, John," I replied. "Welcome back to the farm. Put your stuff in your old room, then get George to drive you out to the lot."

All's well that ends well, as they say.

The men were glad to see John back, too, and at supper they talked, filling him in on what he had missed.

Benny told him about milking the "heifers" and couldn't understand why everybody laughed so much.

"The 'heifers' went on strike," he told John, "and wouldn't let us milk them."

"That's because you're too rough," the Duke rumbled. "John's a farm boy. He'll show you how its done. You have to sque-e-e-e-ze the milk out."

I listened to them laughing together, each comfortable with the division of power within their group. Still, when trouble had brewed, they hadn't been able to stop it or to redirect the dissension to a positive end. They still needed an authority figure with the strength to judge and to act, to issue instructions and to enforce obedience.

Someone once wrote, "Many an army has prospered under a bad commander, but no army has ever prospered under a debating society." I thought of that as I drove home.

LOGS AND SNOW WERE PILING UP in the woods and the men were experiencing difficulty twitching the cut trees out to the barnyard on a drag behind the tractor. The need was great for a horse. The time had come. And just before the problem reached crisis proportions, I noticed an ad in the newspaper: horse for sale. I made a couple of phone calls, sent for the foreman, arranged for a vet to come along, and headed the old truck for a farm on the eastern edge of the city.

"It'll be good to have a horse," the Duke said as they drove through town. "Good for the men. Something for them to look after, I mean. Responsibility. Do them good."

I smiled. I knew the horse would be more for the foreman than for anyone else. The Duke had horses in his blood, and it had been years since he'd had one in his care.

"My father gave me a stallion once, you know," he said. "I was twelve years old. Gave him to me and said, 'Okay. Now you take him back in the woods and learn to work him.' "

I had heard that story before, from the men. They were proud of the strength it showed in their leader.

The horse we came to see, a big 12-year-old called Jack, was about 15 hands high and as strong as any horse I had ever seen.

More than that, he had worked in the woods and was trained to haul logs. It isn't always easy to train a horse to haul. An untrained horse harnessed to a load of logs will not necessarily oblige, but Jack seemed perfect for the work we were doing.

Jack was not a pretty horse. He was a common reddish-brown in colour, and he had a big head and heavy legs. He also had a long dark scar on his back withers, but this and a few smaller marks were the only signs of his life in the woods, and his obvious strength was impressive.

The veterinarian walked him around his box stall, then gave him a thorough examination. After that the Duke walked him around the paddock. Finally I had a chance to walk him. We all agreed that this was a pleasant-mannered animal, quick to obey and eager to please.

"Well, what do you think?"

We tried to be objective, but the truth was we were, one and all, half in love at first sight.

The owner explained that he hadn't any use for Jack any more, though he hated to let him go. The price was right. The vet was satisfied. So we backed the truck into a bank and loaded Jack aboard.

Back at the farm, the men were all waiting. They had cleaned a stall and lined it with burlap bags, and they had filled the manger with nice, clean hay. As one resident said, it was like having a young mother come home with her firstborn.

Bursting with pride and pleasure, the Duke led Jack off the truck and into the barn, followed by the men all in a bunch, all with their hands out ready to give the horse a little pat on the rump.

I would have liked to stay and admire Jack for the rest of the day, too, but duty called and I returned to my office, followed by a resident called Slim.

"Major," Slim said, "I'd like to drive Jack in the woods. I used to work on a farm, and I loved the horses."

"Well," I said, "you're big enough to handle him, so if you've had experience with horses ... all right. I'll put Jack in your charge. You'll drive him. You'll also clean him and feed him."

Slim left the office happy as a school boy who has just made the football team. The next day Duke and I visited nearly every farm along the St. John River from Woodman's Point to Hampstead in search of harness. When we returned, we had the car almost full, some donated and some bought for a few dollars. Jack was fitted out with all the harness he would need: collar, bridle, back strap, traces, and a whiffletree.

The next morning Slim harnessed his horse, found a chain to fasten the logs to the whiffletree, and proudly drove Jack to the woods.

Once at the place where the crews were cutting, he backed Jack up to a log, secured the chain, and confidently shook the reins.

Jack braced against the collar, tightened the traces and chain ... and reared straight up on his hind legs!

"Whoa, boy," Slim soothed, and Jack came down onto all fours.

Slim started him off again.

This time Jack reared up and came down with a jerk, propelling the log (and Slim) on a straight line for the farm as fast as he could go. As he picked up speed on the down-grade, Slim had to let go of the reins, and the horse, with Slim whooping behind him, never stopped galloping till he got to the barn.

Slim skidded into my office. "That horse is crazy!" he howled. "He's too much for me!"

Eventually I got a coherent story out of Slim. "Well, then, let's take the horse back to the woods and see what Langille can do with him," I suggested. "Maybe he just needs someone with a lot of experience to straighten him out."

Slim stuck to his opinion, but Jack stood quietly while I removed the chain from around the log, and he went just as quietly when Slim threw the reins over his back and led him to the woods again.

The Duke hooked Jack to a log. "Now," he said, "let's see you pull."

Again Jack pushed against the collar till he felt the weight—and went straight up onto his hind legs!

"All right," the Duke roared. "If you want to walk like a man, then sit like one."

With that he pulled on the reins with all his great strength and forced the horse back on his haunches.

Jack had met his master.

"Now," the Duke said, very gently, "get up and act like a horse."

With the horse on his legs again, the Duke walked to his head and said, still gently but firmly, "Come, Jack, let's see you pull."

And pull Jack did.

After a few feet the Duke moved out in front and Jack followed to where the log was to be yarded.

The men who had been watching these events, were astonished. "Well!" somebody muttered. "Did you ever see the like! He handled that situation just like a duke!"

People had to try to remember Elton Langille's real name after that; while he was on the farm he was never called anything but Duke.

When two or three more logs had been yarded and Jack knew he could haul the load, Duke turned him over to Slim, and Jack acted like the quiet horse they all expected he would be.

But I found these events puzzling. I was pleased that Duke had taken the horse in hand, but I couldn't shake the feeling that something was not right. Jack was a pleasant-tempered horse. He had no mean steak. It was very odd that he had behaved in such an obstinate and bad-tempered way. I picked up the phone and called Jack's previous owner.

There was a long silence at the other end of the line.

"Yes, well," the farmer began at last, "you see, Major ... when Jack worked in the woods there—hauling ... there was this big crew. And you know what men are. Weekends ... well, you see ... maybe they got into the rum or something ... anyway, they'd have these hauling contests, see? They'd hitch Jack up to a load, and he'd try. He'd try hard. But eventually the load would get too heavy for him. Then they'd yell and pull on the bridle, and beat him. And him straining every muscle!

"Well, sir, maybe he'd move the load or maybe he wouldn't.

But he didn't like it. No, sir, he didn't like it! So after a year or so he got so bad-tempered he bit one of them.

"They were going to shoot him, Major. Nobody'd keep a horse that bit his handlers. But I had a little work for a horse, and a big pasture, so I bought him, and he's been with me seven years, good as gold. I would've thought he'd forgot all about that. I thought he'd do good for you. Only made up my mind to let him go when I seen you'd take good care of him.... I suppose you'll want to bring him back now."

"Oh, I don't think that will be necessary," I said.

Of course not! Jack was already one of the family. After all, you don't return the baby just because he cries.

After that Jack yarded logs for five or six years. Then, because of his age and the hard work he had done, he retired to the pasture to take the rest of his life easy and enjoy the fuss the residents made of him.

CHAPTER FIVE

Building the Barn

MY NOTES FOR SPRING, 1969 INCLUDE "started our scrounging of second-hand lumber [for the new barn] through the kindness of contractors who were dismantling buildings."

In 1970, I wrote: "Through many contacts, the farm was able to obtain many truckloads of second-hand materials from the city.

"Started preparing ground for the construction of new barn."

For 1971, "Started construction of barn. Completed the barn in December. From the city we had picked up boards, planks, windows, doors large and small, wire mesh to go in the cement, equipment for inside the barn. The main cost was the cement and roofing. All other items were second-hand or factory rejects. The barn, 40 feet by 64 feet, we were informed by Government engineers, would cost between $35,000 and $40,000. We completed the barn, including the [electrical] wiring, for $3,884."

For 1972, "We moved into the new barn.

"One of the most rewarding tasks undertaken by the residents of the farm was the construction of the barn."

JUST ABOUT THE FIRST THING anybody noticed at Lonewater Farm was the old barn. It had stood a long time, and like an old man with rheumatism, it had finally developed a lean to the west that was a wonder to the whole community. How long were the poles that braced it going to withstand the pressure? I thought not very long, so one winter day I called the farm foreman and all the men who were experienced in carpentry into the Manor House lounge and told them I was going to build a new barn. My reward was a buzz of interest.

Using a large portable blackboard I drew out the size and shape I had in mind: 40 by 64 feet. I explained that I was pretty sure I could obtain douglas fir trusses at a very reasonable price from a building that was going to be torn down. These trusses were 40 feet long, 10 inches wide, 3 inches thick, doubled and braced. "Should make a good barn," I said. The residents agreed and began to offer many ideas of their own.

The discussion went on for some time. Then the meeting adjourned to the farmyard to survey the building site I had chosen. Everyone agreed it was a first-class site, as water would drain away in all directions but would not contaminate the grounds or the well.

The next day I drove to Fredericton to call on the Minister of Health and ask the Department to finance the barn. Dr. Carten, who agreed there was a great need for a new barn, went with me. The Minister called in his deputy and the Department's engineers.

The meeting went like this: first, I presented my plan without mentioning a price. The engineers did a few rough calculations and muttered, "About $40,000." The Minister shook his head, pursed his lips, and stated categorically, "I haven't got that kind of money. Not for a barn. Not this year." I said, "Take one zero off the estimate and I'll build the barn for that." They all yelled, "What! You must be crazy! You couldn't build a tarpaper shack for $4,000!"

I thought I was going to be committed to the Provincial myself, right there and then. But I stuck to my guns and insisted that I could and would build a barn for $4,000. The Board of Directors gave permission to build the barn but we were not granted financial assistance. As it turned out we came in under the estimate by $268.

Back at the farm, I got hold of the Duke. "We have a lot of scrounging to do," I said. "We'll start tomorrow and see what we can get in the way of doors, windows, boards, timbers, and thing else we can find."

Just when I was building up Lonewater Farm into a

well-founded, safe environment for my men, the City of Saint John was renewing its centre, rapidly razing its old heart to make way for a new one. More than a little of the old heart went up the Nerepis to be reincarnated as barns and houses.

At the time of starting the barn, the old fish plant on the longshore (now Chesley Drive) was coming down. I looked up the contractor on the job and offered to bring in men to help if I could have the lumber.

"Sure," the contractor said. "You can have the floor planks off both floors if you want to take them up."

Just then the contractor was called away to the job.

I looked at the floor boards. "He thinks these planks are spiked down," I said to Duke, "but I don't think they are. Just slip out to the car and bring in a little shovel you'll find in the trunk. Then we'll pry between the planks and see if we can lift them.... But don't let anyone see you do it."

I was right. No nails. No spikes. Each plank was simply laid on the floor joists.

I called out to the contractor that I would bring men down after dinner to remove the floor boards. By that time the contractor's men would be through for the day and the farm crew wouldn't be in their way.

"Okay," the contractor agreed, not paying much attention. "Whatever you like."

So that evening the crew arrived with the van and the 1-ton truck, along with my car, and tools for the job. In no time they had loaded the truck twice with 3-inch planks 8 inches wide and various lengths from 12 to 16 feet.

Of course the contractor had never dreamed that the job could be done so fast, and when he arrived next day with his crew, the floors were gone and there was nowhere for his men to stand. As they say ... mad, or what! Scroungers sometimes have to stay out of some people's way for awhile.

Two days later I spotted a store being demolished. From that site I got windows and more planks.

Then the building that had the coveted trusses, the old feed mill on City Road, came down. I offered to buy the trusses, delivered, for $800, if I could also have all the planks and boards and twelve timbers, 12 inches wide by 16 feet long, that had been treated with creosote. They were reported to be 75 years old and as solid as the day they were cut. (I could see a use for them later—I was always looking ahead.)

The barn was built, not from drawings but from a model. I made the first model truss. Then the residents finished the design to scale.

The foundation was eight concrete pyramids on each side, each pyramid 3 feet in the ground on a base 3 feet square. Each pyramid was 1.5 feet high. Into each pyramid a vertical, 3 by 9 plank 12 feet long was secured. The rest of the frame was fastened to these upright planks. The trusses were placed in U's that protruded a foot above the main posts. They fitted so snugly that one of the men could crawl up to unfasten the chain that lifted them before any spikes were driven to secure them.

When the carpenters were ready for the trusses, I had Irving Equipment bring in a big crane, which they did for half the regular price to assist the farm. The supplier of cement and gravel also gave me a good deal.

Now the barn was ready to be boarded in—with 3-inch planking, all scrounged.

When the barn roof was boarded in and the windows, that all matched, had been put in place, I took Duke and set out to scrounge again. This time we were looking for stanchions to hold the cows in their stalls.

After visiting a few old barns up the St. John River we found what we wanted, a cow barn in retirement.

“Of course,” the farmer said. “Take all you want. There are 24 stalls in there. Not all the stanchions are complete, but you can probably fix them up.”

I drove right back to Lonewater and asked Duke to take a couple of men in the truck and go back up-river for the stanchions.

“And be sure to remind the old farmer to visit us when the barn is finished,” I said.

Next I called the Department of Agriculture in Fredericton and asked them two questions: how wide should the trench behind the cattle be, and how far should the stanchions be from the trench. After a long search in the books an assistant deputy minister reported back that the trench should be wide enough for the chain used to clean it out, and the distance would depend on the breed of cattle.

I didn't want the cows' heads sticking out past the line from the main doors up the length of the barn, so they went with that and started to pour the floor. (I had purchased a small cement mixer for $300, and we ran power from the old barn.) Old wire coat hangers, rods of iron, and found metal went into the mix for strength, and in a few days the floor was poured.

The plan provided stalls for 21 cattle and four calf pens, as well as stabling for three horses, and a tack room. Both cows and horses faced into the barn. I thought, "Too many people walk into a barn and only see the rear end of the animals."

The stables were constructed with a strong gate at the front of each stall to which the manger was attached. Each gate was secured by large hinges and a heavy latch. The design ensured that the horses could be released fast, in case of fire, and driven straight out through the big doors.

It had taken a while, but nothing more was needed now than hay, straw, feed, and the animals.

On moving day, January 1972, there was ice between the barns. I was ready with sand, which the men spread all over the area, especially on the path between the two buildings.

Then I directed everyone to form two lines so that the cattle could walk between two rows of men and understand what was required of them.

"Be sure and hold the line," I said, "so the cows won't get onto the ice and hurt themselves."

Duke led the oldest cow out first, and the others followed in their accustomed order right to the new barn and into their new stalls. By this time the farm had nine cows and two steers.

All went well till a frisky young steer, almost full grown, took a few breaths of fresh winter air, put his head down, and kicked his back legs up in sheer enjoyment. Just like a kid on an outing, he jumped and bucked his way up the line. The men naturally leapt out of the way of his flying hooves. Even so, the line would have held had he not turned and faced a couple of them, lowered his head to display his horns, and let it be known he thought they ought to move.

A gap appeared. The steer rushed through, bucked a couple of times—and crash! Down on the ice.He recovered, got back on the sand, looked around, and then rushed toward the new barn to see where the other cattle had gone.

At the same time I was standing by the new door. As the steer ran by, I grabbed him by the horns and kept him going the right way into the barn. Still holding the horns I led the steer to the last stanchion and said, "Lock him in."

"Wow!" the men exclaimed. "That Major sure knows how to wrangle cattle! He should've been a cowboy!"

THE CATTLE AND HORSES had quarters in the new barn; the hens, goats, and newly-added pigs were housed elsewhere.

Near the Manor House there was a small unused building, which I kept in mind for a pigsty. Eventually I asked a resident carpenter known as "the Cat" (because he was quick on his feet) to take the tractor and move the little building to a location I had chosen. Once moved, the building was to be set up on a rock foundation and divided into three pens.

While the Cat carried out his assignment with his usual competence, the Duke and I visited a farm upriver and bought ten piglets for $11 each. The piggery became another money-maker for the farm, but not without its ups and downs along the way, like all the other undertakings.

Everyone knows that it is bad policy to become emotionally involved with one's farm animals—in this case, pigs. Anyone who has ever done it also knows that it is not possible to raise piglets without becoming emotionally involved; they are far too cute and funny. Lonewater Farm's pigman was not an exception.

Pigman looked after his piglets, kept them warm and clean, fed them only the best of pig rations (unless scraps are boiled they can be bad for pigs) and, at first, all went well.

When the first litter was a couple of months old, I bought another ten, and Pigman was delighted. Then one day he

The new barn near completion.

hurried to my office with one of the new piglets in his arms. “Major,” he cried, “this little fellow is sick!”

I immediately called the vet in west Saint John. “All right,” I said as he hung up, “Dr. Waite will see you. You get ready and I’ll find somebody to drive you.”

Pigman hurried, but just as they reached the animal hospital, the piglet died.

Pigman cried all the way back to the farm. There he dug a small, deep hole and buried the little fellow near the pig pen.

THEY CRIED OVER ARMY, TOO.

The three milk cows each produced a calf. Then, when the calves were old enough, the Government Vet advised me to begin breeding Herefords for beef. So, over a period of years, Lonewater Farm built up a stock of 21 head, while retaining three Guernseys for milking.

The first part-Hereford born was a bull calf. He had the large white face of a Hereford, short legs, big brown eyes, and a short, fat body. The residents called him “Army” because he was born on November 11th.

Army became a pet.

He would roll under the corral fence and follow the men to

the fields, happy to stay with them all day. In the evenings he would go fishing with them where Goose Creek joins the Nerepis. The men would build a fire, Army would lie down beside it, and the fishermen would lean against him for a chair-back as they held their lines. Every now and then they would give him a friendly pat. When Army went away in the big cattle truck, some of them cried openly.

I never claimed to be a cowboy, as the men maintained, but I had a way with animals—probably because they knew I wasn't afraid of them.

JUST BEFORE SHE LEFT to move her belongings from Halifax, Annie asked me if he would feed her dog, a big German shepherd, while she was away. She kept this dog in a large compound surrounded by a six-foot, chain-link fence.

Being very fond of dogs, I agreed.

"He's ugly," she warned. "You'll have to reach in quick and put his dish just inside the gate. If you don't, you'll never get the pan back again."

The next morning I went out with food and water for the dog.

I opened the gate and in a loud voice said, "Sit."

The dog sat.

"Now," I said, "if you want your food, stay."

The dog stayed.

I carried the food into a corner and then said, "Come and eat." The dog walked to the dish, devoured the food and drank the water. When he had finished, I bent down and called the dog to come to me for a pat.

Annie was astounded, on her return, to find her dog walking around the farm at my heel. He was a good dog, if you weren't afraid of him.

But of all the farm animals, the horses were my favourites. Jack, of course, was a general favourite, and there were boarders from time to time, but my own horse (well-named Satan) held a special place in my heart.

Satan used to pull the sloven when the crops were being taken in or there was other work for a farm wagon; otherwise he ranged free in the farmyard.

Unlike Jack, Satan was hard to handle. When he was working, it usually took the Duke to manage him. He was big, strong, and dark with the powerful neck of a stallion—he had not been gelded till he was five. I had no trouble with him.

The German shepherd on guard at the Major's office.

Satan always knew when someone was afraid of him. Then, look out!

Benny, who took pride in his work in the barn and generally enjoyed it, was in mortal terror of Satan.

One noontime, when Satan was just hanging around the farmyard, Benny hurried across the open space to the dining hall. Satan ran after him. Benny took to his heels. Satan snorted and followed. Benny leapt the fence into the pasture and set up such a howl that he brought me and half the men on the place from their lunch to see what the devil was going on.

The next day Satan chased Benny again.

The third day he waited behind the Farm House for Benny to come out. Every few minutes he could be seen poking his head around the corner to see if Benny was coming.

Benny also poked his head out from time to time. At last,

thinking that the coast was clear, he set out at a good clip to cross the yard, but about half way across he felt a huge, dark presence coming up fast behind him. With a terrible roar he took off like greased lightning.

I confined Satan to the pasture after that. Benny's rehabil-

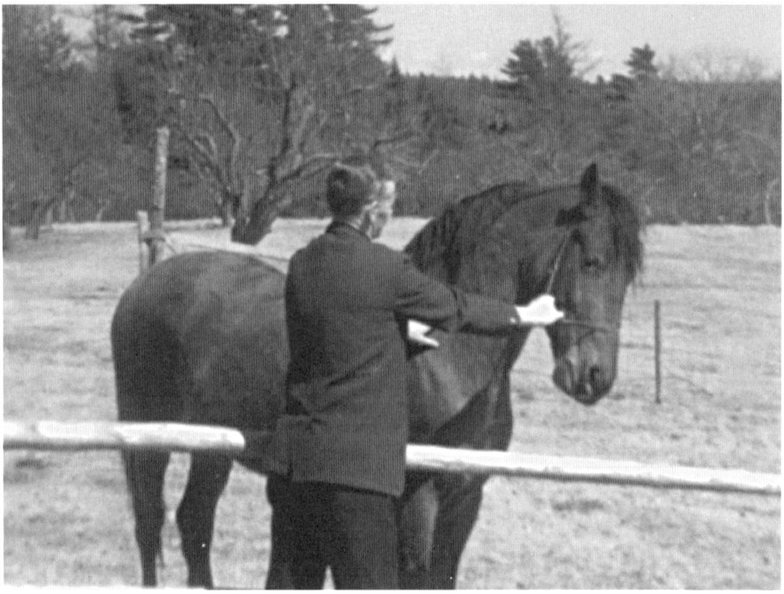
The Major had a special love for Satan and could handle him like no one else.

itation didn't include being harassed by an enormous horse for its amusement.

Satan had at least one other encounter with a human opponent at the farm.

One of the residents, thinking himself something of a horseman, insisted on putting his hand under Satan's halter against his cheek. I tried to warn the fellow, but too late. Satan opened his mouth, tightening the halter against the man's hand, and bolted for the apple orchard, where he galloped around the trees dragging his victim with him.

I caught him and confined him to the barn, but I felt sure that Satan was chuckling in his stall as I left.

Satan often had companions during his idleness—race horses resting at the farm, or mares in foal being boarded there. One day he took two of them out for a little jaunt.

I liked to ride Satan when we both needed exercise, and on a pleasant autumn afternoon, on one of our rambles, I stopped at the Whistle Stop for ice cream. I bought two cones—one for me and one for Satan, and we stood outside the shop enjoying the treat. Some boys came along. What? Was that horse really licking an ice cream cone? Wow! Could they try?

Satan condescended to accept more treats from them, along with pats and murmurs of approval. In fact, Satan enjoyed an orgy of ice cream and popularity.

Early next morning the phone rang. "Hey, Major," an excited voice yodelled. "This is the Whistle Stop. There's three horses down here. We think they're waiting for ice cream!"

Not only had Satan jumped the fence to go to the store, but he had persuaded two others to go with him. Either he was a Napoleon among horses, or he could communicate the idea of ice cream to them—neither of them had ever tasted it before.

Satan's mischief resulted in close confinement in the pasture with the cows and goats, which may have been a relief to the men but did little for the animals. Not even cows like to be cooped up with a holy terror; billy-goats resent it deeply.

The cook used to dump potato peelings into the pasture as a treat. The cows liked the peelings but rarely had their share, because Billy would drive them away.

Billy considered himself field foreman—until Satan came among them. That day changed the order of things forever. The peelings arrived. Billy drove off the cows and settled down to eat. Across the field Satan was watching proceedings. He shook his head, snorted, and sauntered over to see what was going on.

Billy held his ground.

Satan just stood there, waiting for this little runt to get out of the way. But Billy tucked his chin down and charged.
Satan recovered from his surprise just as Billy made his first, and last, pass. As Billy went by, Satan nipped the goat's tail between his teeth driving poor Billy pell mell ahead of him across the pasture.

The squeals of anguish were heart-rending.

Satan wasn't bad—just bored. He had too much strength and energy for a life of ease, that was all. So in the winter Duke

The Major feeding some of the farm's goats.

took him into the woods to yard logs. They both enjoyed themselves.

"That Satan!" Duke would say, and shake his head. "That fellow has more guts than any horse I ever saw. Yarding logs up them steep hills is hard work, and the boys sometimes try to make him rest halfway up, but he never will. Not till he gets to the top!"

Satan was a fine example to the men and worthy of his place on the roster of farm employees—much more worthy than some of the human types who came later.

CHAPTER SIX

Tranquility

BESIDES THE BARN-RAISING AND THE CARE of animals, besides the wood-cutting and all the other undertakings at Lonewater, we also organized crop-growing.

Potatoes, hay, and oats were chief—that is, they produced the largest quantities; but the gardens grew enough vegetables to supply the needs of the kitchen in summer, and some to store for winter; and there were usually apples to give away to the Protestant Orphanage and to the Sisters of Charity. For several years there were potatoes enough to sell (before the population of the farm grew to upwards of 50 men) and in gardening season there were always vegetables to give to friends. The doctor, for example, found himself in a quandary over vegetables: he did not want to receive a single thing in return for the care he provided, but the men wanted to say thanks and often bypassed his protests by placing gifts from the garden in his car.

Many hands make light work of gardening, especially if they are gardeners' hands. If not … well, some of the hands that gardened at Lonewater had never been much accustomed to it.

The man they called "Sundown," for instance, was very willing, but, sent out to weed the potatoes, he left all the mustard plants in the ground.

He was called Sundown because, being very tall, he walked with his head forward, making him look to someone standing behind as though his head (the sun) were sinking behind his shoulders. The Duke named him, of course.

"Why didn't you take the mustard out too?" the Duke asked.

"Everybody knows mustard goes with potatoes!" Sundown replied.

"Not this mustard," the Duke rumbled. "If we don't get rid of it now, while the plants are small, we'll be up to our ears in it. And it'll grow up tough and prickly. You'll need thick leather gloves in a week or two."

"I didn't know that!" Sundown exclaimed.

The only really experienced gardener they had was Eddy. He became grounds keeper in charge of lawns and flowers.

Eddy was also de facto morale officer.

Once the herd of cattle had grown to fill the available stalls, the farm's own hay fields could not keep up with the demand, and I was always looking for standing grass to scrounge or buy. One summer we hayed a property at Public Landing a few miles up the St. John River.

Having worked hard all day, the men relaxed over their supper, thinking that they could now shower and take life easy for awhile, maybe go swimming in the river.

But ... "It's such a beautiful evening," I said. "It would be a shame to leave the rest of the hay out in the field overnight to become damp. Let's make one more trip and bring it in."

The haymakers groaned, but they climbed back in the truck, and off they went.

Eddy waited on the steps of the Farm House.

When the light faded and the men had still not returned, he armed himself with a powerful flashlight, and went on waiting till he heard the truck coming along the road. Then, just as the truck turned into the lane, he switched on the flashlight, started up the lawnmower, and was busy marching up and down the lawn when the lights of the truck swept over him.

"You guys are lucky," he called out, wiping nonexistent sweat from his brow. "I have another two hours to go!"

In haying time, I took the men up and down the rivers from Hampton to Hampstead and back again. Eventually the Provincial Hospital's Annex (a farm where able, long-term patients worked with animals and grew crops) was closed, and for a couple of years Lonewater hayed there.

On one of those summer occasions,I sent a convoy of equipment to the Annex, a distance of about 20 miles. The farm truck pulled the hay conditioner, the big tractor pulled the mower, and the pony tractor came along behind with a rake.

When I thought the convoy should have arrived, Duke and I drove down to see how the haymaking was going. Disaster! The pony tractor driver had taken a detour, rake and all, to the liquor store, and provided himself with a bottle of vodka. He was immediately discharged and taken to a halfway house in the city.

That same evening, a former contractor for the Annex's hay waited till the men from Lonewater had cut a field; then he came in after they had gone home, baled up all the cut grass, and removed it to his own barn.

The next year a contractor, who was taking down the old barns at the Annex, made off with a thousand bales that belonged to Lonewater. I complained, but Fredericton said it was only hay; forget it.

In spite of these ups and downs, there was always enough hay at the farm to supply the animals through the winter. Sometimes there was hay to sell.

LIFE AT THE FARM WENT ON in this successful, even fairly tranquil, way for six years.

The Hitching Post, a weekly paper printed by a resident for farm use, on Saturday, December 28, 1974 published a list of significant events of that year:

"JANUARY: Record sales of pulpwood ... [Pulp was hauled to the Irving Pulp and Paper mill in west Saint John. Irvings were very good, offering to help in any way they could, even to advancing financial aid to Lonewater's woods operations if it should be needed.]

"FEBRUARY: Residents of Lonewater Farm played a major role in maintaining access to main roads during record snowfalls throughout the month of February.

"MARCH: Blackie the dog believed to have fallen to his death through thin ice.

"Don, the assistant-manager, terminated employment with the Farm. [By this time, I had some hired help: an assistant-manager, a clerk-typist, a bookkeeper, and counsellors to provide someone on duty at all times.]

"APRIL: Construction begins on McLaughlin Hall.... [McLaughlin Hall was another of the Major's "$4,000" buildings. It contained new kitchen and dining facilities.]

"MAY: E. B. named Sportsman of the Year.

"JUNE: Major E. A. Flewwelling elected Mayor of the City of Saint John.

"JULY: A black bear is captured outside the Farm House.

"AUGUST: Sam McCallum joins staff.

"SEPTEMBER: Farm harvests heavy potato crop. Sadie leaves staff.

"OCTOBER: Farm loses apple crop to early frost.

"NOVEMBER: Residents participate in provincial general election.

"DECEMBER: Residents play an active and helpful role in contributing to the Empty Stocking Fund.

"Power is finally installed in the Pool Hall. [The men wanted a pool table, and I thought a 'Pool Hall' without alcohol would be an excellent place for them to learn they could enjoy the game cold sober, a lesson many of them would need when they went back to the world.]"

Successful, and on the surface fairly tranquil, the farm had been operating long enough by 1974 to provide a source of stories beginning "Do you remember ...?" whenever ex-residents got together.

"Do you remember the time the provincial forester came to cruise the farm woods and told the Major to build a road 30 feet wide and clear-cut half the property?" [Some exaggeration often crept in.]

"Yeah, the Major sure wasn't having any of that!"

"No way. Spoiling our nice farm, and making roads for guys to get in and start fires."

One thing that we always worried about was fire.

IN THE SUMMER OF 1972 the woods were very dry and fire broke out near the village of Martinon. Before long the smell of fire was everywhere, blowing over the city, lying on the rivers ... this was a big one.

I was just leaving home when I smelled the smoke, and it

didn't take me long to get out to the farm and mobilize the men. I always saw that some of them were trained to fight fires in case of conflagration in the farm woods, so they already knew what to do. In no time they were organized into three-man crews each comprised of a man with a chain saw, one with a shovel and an axe, and one with a water-backpack.

That day everyone volunteered. Nobody would ever hang back at a time like that. Fighting fires is a thing you do in New Brunswick. It's hot, stifling, hard, and dangerous; but it's elemental—man against nature, man with his back to the wall, man at his best.

Every man who was strong enough to stand the rigours of the job went to Martinon. They loaded their equipment into my car, into the van and the truck, and roared off down the lane, down Campbell Road, down the River Road, ready for any forest fire and what it could do … till they were stopped by a police officer.

"Who is in charge of fighting the fire?" I shouted.

"Nobody knows," the policeman shouted back. "They're arguing over whether it's the Saint John Fire Department or the Forest Rangers."

The Lonewater crews froze with their mouths open, but I snapped right back, "Then if any volunteers turn up, tell them Major Flewwelling is in charge and to report to me."

The fire was working east toward a cluster of houses.

"We'll move down the old River Road as far as the houses that are in the path of the fire," I ordered. "Then we'll work our way back toward it, cutting down everything in our path and dropping it inward, toward the fire, so it can't use the tops to cross our fire break."

The men nodded. They knew what I meant. Many of them had fought fires before and knew the game plan: if it's in the ground, bury it; if it's in the underbrush, douse it; if it's in the tops, run like hell.

Already volunteers were gathering; big, Irving-owned bulldozers were on the way; other businesses were mustering men and equipment. And the police told them all to report to me.

That fire burned for three days. It burned over 200 acres of woodland. But not a man was badly injured or a house lost.

By midnight of the first day the Forest Rangers finally established jurisdiction and I turned over to them about 200 men and three bulldozers, but they said everything was so well organized they would like the Lonewater crews to carry on.

We did. We stayed the full three days. Bill Kirk, who ran a store in the neighbourhood, kept us supplied with soft drinks, as cold as he could deliver them; and Mrs. Kirk and the other women of the village never stopped making sandwiches from store supplies. Bill Kirk himself drove out with this food every hour on the hour. And everybody within reach offered whatever they had that might be needed.

The men who fought that battle learned a great deal about their own worth and the worth of others. Three days of strenuous cooperative effort—without a bath, without clean clothes, eating on the run, sleeping only when they dropped—did them a world of good. After that they were battle-scarred veterans and walked taller.

And as icing on the cake, besides basking in the praise and gratitude of the community, the Forest Rangers took their names and hours on the job, and the Province paid them.

WHILE SITTING IN MY OFFICE in the evening I could often hear the men in the lounge, telling one another stories.

"Do you remember all them deer that used to come out around the farm in the early spring of the year?"

"Yeah. Pretty things, deer. Funny big eyes, they have."

"Specially when you catch them in the lights of your car at night."

"Oh, my God, yes! I hit one once, poor thing. Broke its neck."

"Were you there the time Benny was coming out of the barn just about dusk and this big buck was standing in the yard looking around?"

"No. What happened?"

"What happened! Benny, he went straight up in the air about four feet and came down squawking! You talk about run! Him and the deer both!"

"You know, the Major could've filled the freezer with deer meat any time he wanted, if he wanted to. I mean, legal. We could've shot them in hunting season. Instead of that, he puts up them red discs that mean you have to ask permission to hunt on the property. Not that the Major ever gave permission. Nobody ever asked him, I don't think. Everybody knew he liked the woods and the animals. He always said the no-hunting signs was there so's the men wouldn't get shot by hunters when we was out in the woods working. And that would've been part of it, for the Major was never a man to put up with lies or to tell them himself. But he liked the chance to save the animals, too."

"Oh, yes. He never liked us keeping the wild animals for pets, do you remember? Though if a man caught something and liked it, he wouldn't say to get rid of it. Maybe sometimes he should've. Like them two mink that died because the dogs wouldn't stop barking at them. And the raccoon somebody had—who was that? The Major made him let the 'coon go. Right thing, too."

"Do you remember when we seen the tracks of a cougar? Big one. No mistake. Somehow the Game Warden got wind of it and was gonna shoot it. 'No,' says the Major, 'if anybody shoots that cougar, I will.' Always wondered what he meant by that. Do you think he would really've shot it if it came around?"

"Naw. Not the Major. Not unless it was after a calf or something; then he might. Them cougars, you know, they're very scarce. Hardly anybody ever seen one, even their tracks."

"You ever seen one?"

"No. Not me. But I seen a bear. Out there. On the farm. He was right outside my bedroom trying to get in through a window. God's truth. That was the time the Major got the game warden to bring in a big live-trap and we caught the bear and took him away deep in the woods."

"Bear came ambling towards some of us working out in the back field once. Now there was a bear. Four hundred pounds if he was an ounce. Come in for some apples. There was a few trees just in back of us, you see. Yes, sir ... young fellow from the North Shore, there ... I think it was ... anyway he just happened to have a camera with him—always taking pictures of stuff—and, well sir, he kept snapping pictures of that bear till it was not more than 16 feet away. Then he took out of there, and us all after him.

"Yeah. But now if you ask me ... and don't say, 'Well, we didn't ask you ..."

"No. You go right ahead. And if it's the one about the time you and Relic was working out to Dexter's gravel pit ... "

"That's her. And some of you may not remember the time ...

"You see, the Major got this job for some of the boys clearing brush out at the gravel pit. Relic was there, for he drove the tractor. And there was me and some other fellows—I forget all who. And they brought in a big bulldozer to knock down the trees ahead of us.

"Now this was in the spring of the year before the leaves was full out on the trees, but the woods was full of birds singing and that, and it was real nice in there—before the tractor and dozer came on the scene.

"Well, anyway, we all set to work, and we're knocking down trees and clearing them away like good fellows, when this little bitch fox appears up a side-hill that Relic is on with the tractor, and her running back and forth, back and forth, like she's gone crazy or something.

" 'I believe that fox is trying to tell us something,' " says Relic, and off he goes—on foot, now—running up to the top of the hill to see what's up.

"Well, sir, it didn't take a genius ... and that was a good thing, for Relic wasn't one ... well, none of us was, was we! But we soon seen what happened! Here's this poor little fox had her den buried by the dozer, and her with three or four pups in it.

"Well, we all set to work, and in no time at all we had the den clear, and then we all stood back and watched the mother trotting back and forth with the pups, one by one, moving them to some new place to live, poor thing.... Didn't seem to blame us. Seemed like she was grateful to us for coming to the rescue.... Pretty little animals, foxes."

CHAPTER SEVEN

Turning Point

THERE IS, IT SEEMS, NO END TO THE STORIES, the reminiscences of those men. But the most significant happenings of the year 1974 were outside the area of their perceptions; that is, the two elections and the effects they were to have on Lonewater Farm.

With everything running smoothly at the farm, I felt free to spread my wings a little and was elected Mayor of Saint John. And in Fredericton, the Hatfield government was returned to power. Although it was too early to tell, Lonewater was on a collision course with new philosophies and new personalities.

In November 1973, the farm had been taken over by the Department of Health, and the successful bid for re-election of the Hatfield government meant that the agenda of that government, as it applied to Lonewater, would continue.

"Some know how, but we can do it," might have been my motto for the next few years. I was to be tried almost beyond endurance by those who were convinced they knew how; that they knew, not only how, but how best to do whatever it was needed doing, including running Lonewater Farm. They tried to dictate how to handle the men when in reality they didn't even know how to talk to a man.

In fulfilment of an election promise, the new provincial government planned to set up the New Brunswick Alcohol and Drug Dependency Commission to coordinate and administer all the treatment and rehabilitation centres in the province. Nobody objected to this plan. In fact, both parties had promised to rationalize and improve treatment for alcoholics and drug addicts. In my view the problem arose from too many theorists trying to direct others.

There was also a problem with precipitate action. Long before they were ready with a new administration, Fredericton dissolved the old. Then, since Lonewater and the other centres could not function in limbo, they set up an Interim Commission.

The directors of Lonewater Foundation Inc. resigned as required. The Interim Commission took over. And from that day the farm slid downhill, though I fought every inch of the way to hold our ground.

It was anticipated that the Interim Commission would be replaced in a few months but three years went by. Then the permanent Commission proved to be not much better than the Interim. Both did irreparable harm to the farm.

The Minister of Health asked me to sit as a member of the Interim Board and to submit to the Department the names of people he thought would also be good members. I submitted the names of several businessmen and a doctor, but when the new directors arrived at the farm, where the first meeting was held, the only people I knew were the doctor I had named and a senior civil servant (SCS).

The instructions to the Board were that the Minister of Health would appoint the chairman, but the senior civil servant lost no time in taking over. "Who wants to be chairman?" he said, "I'll take it."

Naturally he would be chairman. He knew all anyone would ever need to know about alcoholism, alcoholics, treatment and rehabilitation of alcoholics, rehabilitation centres and the running of same; he knew how to feed the cat, how to pick water lilies, and what to do with Aunt Aggie's old feather pillows.

He also knew a bit about scrounging, but only for his own benefit. Whenever he visited the farm he went away with something—vegetables, potatoes, apples ... always asked for them, too. Friends of the farm might be offered produce. Some, like the doctors, might be pressed to accept little gifts. The SCS had to ask—and did.

At that time the residents had a supply of pine planks, bought at a discount that could not be repeated, for making picnic tables which they sold for profit. Two of those planks went west, literally, with the SCS. Well, he asked; he was Chairman of the Board (even if self-appointed) so what could anyone do?

Successful in his first attempt, the next time he visited he brought a friend and asked for more planks. Was the friend to have some too? I pointedly mentioned price, but to no avail. Strange that when they went for my jugular a couple of years later, they accused me of taking hay from the farm for my own use!

IN THE DAYS WHEN DR. CARTEN and one assistant ran the programmes for alcoholics from a corner of the Depart-ment of Health, I had no difficulty procuring what I needed, including the ear of the administration. When the Interim Board took over, however, those days of reason and efficiency disappeared forever, and I quickly learned what it means to have enemies in high places—and how to fight them.

About the time of the changeover, I called the Minister of Health for an appointment to discuss an agenda of six improvements to the farm, and asked that Dr. Chalmers and two other ministers from the southern part of the province be present.

When I arrived at the Minister's office for the meeting, the Minister said, "Well, Ed, you called this meeting. You chair it."

Three items were quickly agreed upon.

When the fourth came up, the Minister said, "Take that one up with my staff."

"No," I replied, "if I had wanted to talk to your staff, I would have arranged a meeting with them. I wanted to talk to the people who were responsible to the voters."

One minister, with some pungent language thrown in, suggested I listen to the Minister of Health and get on with it.

At that I put my papers in my briefcase and stood up. "I can hear that kind of language every day at the farm," I said. "I expect better from the Ministers of Her Majesty's Government.... You can read about the rest of the agenda in the newspaper on Monday."

Then I started for the door.

Two of the ministers, one of whom was Dr. Chalmers, jumped up and stopped me.

"Come on, Edis. Don't leave till we finish this," the doctor said. Then, with a few well chosen words, he brought the others down from their perch.

I stayed and the whole agenda was approved.

Political blackmail had never been part of my arsenal and I didn't like it, but sometimes there didn't seem to be any alternative. I had to resort to the same tactic to stop an order preventing the hospitals of the province from admitting, for treatment of other problems, a known alcoholic or any person obviously drunk. The order was implemented by the Department of Health over my strong objections.

One Saturday night shortly after, a cook at the farm returned from a visit to his hometown, Fredericton, drunk and sick. A counsellor drove him to the Provincial in Saint John, but they refused to admit him. Then, out of kindness, the counsellor drove him all the way back to Fredericton, a distance of 50 miles, to see his family doctor. The agreement was that the cook would return to the farm by bus on Monday.

On Monday "Cook" went to the bus station at the right time, but the bus was late. He sat down on a bench outside to wait. A chap he knew came along, sat down alongside him, gave him a drink and went into the station to see when the bus was coming. When he returned to the bench, he found that the Cook was dead.

Among the crowd from the farm who went to Fredericton for the funeral, one had a camera with him and, taking advantage of being momentarily alone with the deceased, snapped a couple of pictures. Everyone to his own taste. The point is, that when the film was developed there was another picture of Cook on the same roll, taken the previous Friday, all dressed up for his little holiday.

Again I asked to see the Minister of Health, taking with me the pictures of Cook in my pocket. But by now the Minister knew me pretty well and brought along some reinforcements: the Deputy Minister and two other assistants.

I asked the Minister to put out an order to all hospitals to open their doors to any man or woman suffering from alcoholism, whether drunk or sober, when they needed help that would not be denied to any other citizen of the province.

The Minister and his staff put up determined resistance to tying up beds for such patients. Seeing that I was getting nowhere, I passed around the picture of Cook alive.

"That was our cook on Friday," I said. "Nice, neat-looking fellow, don't you think?"

They all agreed.

"He was refused admittance to the Provincial Hospital a day later," I said, "because he had been drinking.... He was also very sick."

Then I played my ace and passed around the picture of Cook in his coffin.

"Two days later," I said.

"Sensationalism!" they shouted.

"Call it what you like," I said, "but if you don't rescind that order by the end of the week, this story—with the pictures—goes to the press."

It took the death of one man to get the order rescinded.

Along with several other questionable appointments, the Interim Board hired two individuals who were less than useful to the farm. The "programmer" was supposed to design activities for the residents and see that everything was in place for the activities to be carried out. He never did much but cause trouble. The title of the other was Director of Alcoholic Programmes for the Province of New Brunswick.

The new farm programmer was a defrocked priest, who was thrown out of the Church for his "social activities," as I learned after he had departed the scene. Without permission from the Board, or me, he moved a trailer onto the farm with his wife and two children and took up residence not far from the men's quarters.

The other chap, the Director of Programmes for the Province, was the same man who had insulted the Roman Catholic sister who operated a rehabilitation centre for women, cancelled the Order's grants and, with the aid of several women who were working at the Ridgewood Rehab, opened an alternative place for women. Eventually "the director" was fired by the Province. He left for Newfoundland with his secretary. But he was fired from a position there, too, and came back to New Brunswick to be rehired by my nemesis, the Senior Civil Servant, the self-styled Chairman of the Interim Board.

From the beginning, this Senior Civil Servant (SCS) and his appointees were out to get rid of me. Events prove that they worked very hard toward that end. What they did and how they did it are plain. But why they did it is more difficult to understand.

Lonewater Farm was successful. Men left there improved in general health and self-esteem, much better able to fight their addictions than they were when they entered Lonewater's programme. One study showed that 32 per cent of ex-residents were employed in their same job for at least two years after reentering the workforce. Compared to many other institutions, that was a phenomenal record.

There had been no breach of trust, no trouble in the neighbourhood, no dangerous or life-threatening undertakings. And the farm was profitable. At a time when it cost $56 a day to keep a man in hospital and $25 to keep him in jail, it cost less than $1 at the farm.

I was believed to be a Liberal in a time of Conservative rule. Could that have been enough? Were they simply trying to please their political bosses? Probably nobody will ever know.

Still, I was to go; and when I became Mayor of Saint John, my enemies thought they had me. The cry of "patronage" went up. "It's political patronage, when the man can be mayor of the city and still be a paid employee of the province." Patronage was the worst thing a politician could be accused of in those years. Other political "crimes" were mere peccadillos; the unforgivable sin was patronage.

I earned $12,000 a year as mayor, without expenses. A later mayor suggested that her stipend just about paid for the extra clothes she had to buy to keep up appearances.

Never mind that I still put in longer hours at the farm than most men's 40-hour week. And that I spent evenings, weekends, and holidays there as well as being on call around the clock every day. Forget that I still commanded the respect and loyalty of the residents. Apparently, secret meetings between staff from Fredericton and disloyal staff from the farm convened in a diner in Grand Bay. They decided that I had to go.

THE SCS CALLED ON ME in my office at City Hall. His intention was obvious, but he circled around the subject till I stated it for him.

"You want me to resign as farm manager," I said, "but I won't. I like that job."

So this old so-and-so wouldn't resign. Then they'd get me some other way. If they couldn't shame me with charges of patronage, then exposing my theories on rehabilitation ought to do the trick.

Possibly they truly believed my methods were wrong. Possibly they really thought I was running a Siberian gulag and that the residents would be better off sitting on their beds swallowing pills to control their addictions.

Possibly it was the experts' conviction that only those who hold the degrees and speak the jargon can know what a patient needs; or, conversely, the fear that, if someone without formal training in their profession succeeds, then what does that make them?

Men who arrived at the farm from Ridgewood Treatment Centre often said that the farm wasn't a bit like they were told to expect. People at Ridgewood had the impression that it was worse than an army camp, a place where everybody had to work so hard a man was a fool to go there.

To counter that ploy, I invited a pre-eminent expert on addictions and how to treat the addicted to visit the farm. Mr. Cosman was an advisor on addictions to the American Senate, to the Government of Canada, and to the Province of Prince Edward Island.

I gave Mr. Cosman a thorough tour of the farm and we talked for several hours. Afterward, on the drive back to the city, Mr. Cosman remarked that he was very glad to see they were practising the new methods of rehabilitation at Lonewater.

Throughout the western states, he said, and in many in the east, as well as in parts of Canada, they were practising what he considered the best rehabilitation methods. For the alcoholic, he said, the best thing is meaningful work. Forget lecturing. Once in a while lecturing may be useful, but alcoholics already know about alcoholism; lectures go in one ear and out the other.

"Sobriety through productivity," I suggested.

"Exactly. Men look and feel healthier, think more clearly, eat and sleep better. And if you must lecture to them ... well, in the evening, when they are relaxing after a day's work, they are more receptive."

My critics were foiled again. Negative advertising hadn't worked. And there was all that positive advertising being dispensed by men who left Lonewater in control of their lives. One man, who we called Mr. Dress Up, had spent only six months at the farm, and there he was going from AA meeting to AA meeting, extolling the wonders of the help he received at Lonewater.

In December, 1976, the Alcoholic Director of the Department of Health, recommended to the Interim Commission that a programmer be hired to set up regular daytime lectures at the farm. Shades of Bill, the bookkeeper in Annie's day, who exclaimed, "But, Major! These guys are derelicts!" The testimony of drunks wasn't worth a puff of wind off the marsh. Nor was the opinion of other experts worth any more—if they disagreed.The post was filled in February, 1977. After a few weeks of studying the farm's existing programmes in operation, the programmer informed me that he wouldn't change a thing.

Nevertheless, when I returned full-time to the farm having served three years in City Hall, I felt that the atmosphere of the place had changed. But I had no intention of resigning and every intention of working through my problems.

One of the first things I discovered was that while I had been mayor, the farm's canteen books had not been kept correctly. I called in the government auditors. The auditors told me to make out a cheque to myself, as I would for petty cash, and then deposit that cheque to the credit of the canteen, which I did.

The hay business was a little more complicated, but equally innocent. I bought some standing hay for my own use, hired the farm to cut it, and paid in hay—that is, the farm received some of that hay in lieu of money. Although I did skip some steps that accountants find necessary, the farm staff knew all about the deal and approved it.

One day, soon after my return from City Hall, I told the then foreman (not Duke) and the Preacher (as the residents called the programmer) that Mrs. Flewwelling and I were going to spend the weekend in Nova Scotia.

That same weekend, the Preacher, having seen the canteen cheque with my name on it, and knowing about the hay arrangement, scuttled up to Fredericton with his "evidence" of wrongdoing against me. At last, they had me!

The Preacher did not, however, go to the Board. He went directly to the RCMP. Was he acting on orders? Perhaps they knew nothing about it, but no member of the Board of Management of the Alcoholic Commission ever asked me for my side of the story. They gave me no opportunity to defend myself against the allegations; the matter went to court.

CHAPTER EIGHT

Trial

NOVEMBER 10, 1977. A CLEAR, FALL DAY, the kind that one enjoys on the drive to work after a good breakfast and a couple of deep breaths of cold, fresh air.

My drive took me away from the city by way of South Bay and the River Road, through the pleasant villages that line the valley.

The road offered panoramas of the river, a beautiful waterway throughout the year, but particularly so in November, especially looking across the Nerepis Marsh.

I arrived at Lonewater feeling fine. The calm and peace of the place felt good.

I swung into the tasks of the day. First, my morning rounds.

The cows had been milked and were grazing with the horses and ponies. The wood crews were in the saw pit cutting hardwood stove-lengths—everything was so quiet I could hear the saw teeth bite into the wood. In the new wagon shed, that the residents had built over the past summer and early fall, the welding crew were repairing, welding, and painting sections of tubular-steel staging that the farm had contracted to keep in mint condition. House orderlies appeared at doors and windows as they cleaned the houses.

The men waved or nodded good morning to me as I passed. I knew they were happy and healthy, on the road back to sobriety.

I walked through the barn, my pride and joy. As usual it was so clean I hoped someone would come to visit so I could show it off.

The maintenance man was busy checking buildings,

preparing for winter which was just around the corner. "When she comes, we'll be ready," I said with a smile.

In the fine new kitchen and dining room that the residents had built, cooks and helpers, all residents, were cleaning up after breakfast and preparing lunch.

In the storeroom the storeman was checking records and packing rations into a large wire basket.

In the Manor House, where, along with me, the assistant-manager, the foreman (who was now a hired employee), the programmer, and the clerk all had offices, everything was orderly and quiet. The clerk gave me a cheerful good morning.

I checked the mail, wrote up three of four receipts, made a few notes for a meeting with some of the men, and began to think about a big job I had to do that could only be completed when I had replaced the bookkeeper who had recently left. I had not made an annual report since 1974, because the SCS, the Chairman of the Interim Board, had told the bookkeeper it was not required. Now it was required, and I knew it would be a lot of work.

I was at my desk, reviewing in my mind some details of the research into back records that would have to be done, when three RCMP officers entered and handed me a warrant to search for stolen goods hidden on the farm.

"How interesting," I said. "You are really helping me a lot. I am the guest speaker tomorrow night at a Royal Canadian Legion dinner, and I plan to speak on our duty as citizens to support the RCMP."

The Mounties smiled, perhaps ruefully.

"What is it you want to see?" I asked then. "Your warrant says stolen goods hidden here. Let's go and see what we can find."

At that, the two constables walked off to search other rooms, but the corporal in charge stayed in my office.

"No. I'll be going through your books, sir," he said.

I knew then that someone had lied to the judge who issued the warrant, but I opened file cabinets, drawers, and cupboards—even pointed out boxes of old material. I still had no idea what the police were looking for (though I had a pretty good idea of why they were looking) but I had no reason not to cooperate.

"Help yourself," I said. "Our books are the property of the provincial government."

As the corporal settled down at a desk to start going through the records, he said, "Is your wife at home, Major Flewwelling?"

"I believe so," I replied.

"Perhaps you'd like to call her."

I did so immediately.

"Edis!" Mrs. Flewwelling cried, when she heard my voice. "Three or four Mounties have just come, and they're going to search our house!"

"Just cooperate with them," I advised calmly. "They haven't told me what they want, but we have nothing to hide."

What were they looking for? My first guess had been drugs, but they don't look for drugs in ledgers … do they?

Both my wife and I spent a perplexing and uncomfortable morning, and as soon as the police left the farm with a pile of papers, I got on the phone to Fredericton. The Minister of Health was not in her office, so I called my friend the Minister of Finance and asked him if he knew what was going on. "No idea, Ed! But get hold of the Minister of Justice. He's at the opening of the Workers Compensation Board complex in Grand Bay." I went to Grand Bay and found the Minister of Justice. "Good Lord! No idea, Major! But I'll find out and let you know the minute I get back to my desk on Monday!"

I drove home, none the wiser, to find Mrs. Flewwelling very upset. "They searched through everything," she cried. "Cellar to attic. Even the papers about my father's estate!"

"They're looking for something they think we've hidden," I said. "They must be trying to blame me for something … did they take anything from the house?"

"I believe they took a small loose-leaf notebook with them. And they took photos of the house, inside and out!"

(The notebook contained my personal notes on city business and my comments on individuals I had dealt with as mayor. It was returned to me without comment a couple of months later.

I had no knowledge of where it was or of whether any use was made of it while it was out of my hands.)

We spent the rest of that day and the evening trying to figure out what was going on. This must be what it was like to live in a police state. We wondered what our rights were.

Next morning, Friday, November 11, I felt too unsettled to attend the memorial service. Instead, I concentrated on a new subject for my speech.

"But the Mounties were not here on their own," Mrs. Flewwelling said. "Someone had to order them here. And one of them told me they didn't find anything in the house."

Nevertheless, I wrote my speech on the tasks facing the Royal Canadian Legion in a changing world.

On Saturday, following my custom established over the past nine years, I drove to the farm to check on what the men were doing, to organize some of them to keep them busy, and to talk with the programmer.

The programmer couldn't be found, either in the farm buildings or in his trailer, but some of the men told me they had seen him all dressed up to go to the city, they believed to a meeting.

I went into my office and was there only a couple of minutes when the phone rang: the Chairman of the Interim Board. Would I stay at the farm till he drove up from Saint John?

As I hung up the phone, I, "Now I'll find out what the police were after."

Half an hour later the Chairman (the SCS) arrived with two other men, all looking very important.

"In the light of the RCMP action," the SCS pronounced, "I am here to tell you that you are suspended as manager of Lonewater Farm and to warn you not to come back on the farm's land until all this is over."

"By whose authority?" I demanded.

"We had a meeting, and you are suspended as of now," was the only reply.

Then the SCS asked if the programmer was at home.

"I don't know," I answered. "I can call him."

The programmer was at home, and I turned the phone over

to the SCS, who asked the programmer to come down to the office. Two minutes later he arrived in work clothes and high boots.

"The Major has been suspended from the farm," the SCS announced.

The programmer looked and acted very surprised. Later I learned that he had been one of four at the secret meeting held at the Admiral Beatty Hotel, where the farm and my position were the only subject. He should have been an actor; at the time, I believed he was surprised.

"You will be acting manager," the SCS told him.

Again amazement. "Oh!" he said. "Oh! Well, yes, I can handle it."

The three visitors left then, and I took the new acting manager out into the yard to talk to him without being overheard.

"What's going on here, Peter?" I demanded.

"I don't know."

"Somehow you are mixed up in this. If you felt the farm wasn't being run right, why didn't you come to me? Instead, I must now believe what I didn't want to believe: that when I took a weekend off and went to Nova Scotia, you went to Fredericton to report on the farm and me."

Peter didn't reply, but his acting wasn't as good as it had been.

Later he button-holed Duke and demanded suspiciously, "How did the Major know I went to Fredericton?"

"Oh!" Duke said with a laugh, "you only have to walk into an office up there and the Major hears about it. He has more friends than you will ever know."

That morning, though, the Preacher found out that I didn't number him among his friends.

"I believe loyalty goes both ways," I said to him. "Whenever someone asked me how you were doing—including the Board—even though I knew you weren't doing much, that you had no programme beyond the one I set up, and that you held very few interviews ... even though I have always had to discuss your work with you and show you what needed to be done, to be loyal

I always told people you were doing just fine. I see I made a mistake. I am surprised and disappointed."

I turned my back on the chagrined Preacher and went for a walk with the Duke.

Duke blew his top. "I told you that bloody Preacher was planted here!" he roared. "They want to get rid of you. And the foreman they have now is working with him. Keeping notes when you come and go! Writing down who you talk to! Who you do business with...."

I went home.

Early in the evening I called the Minister of Health.

"My God!" she said. "It sounds like those two fellows the Commission hired—that new one in Fredericton ... what's his name? And the Regional Director in Saint John."

The Regional Director had a master's degree, a year's experience, and a penchant for using six-syllable words.

"If you ask me, the Interim Chairman knows a lot about what's going on," I told her.

The Minister replied that she was going out for the evening but would call Fredericton right away and get back to me.

Since it was Saturday night, I was sure she would have a problem finding her staff, but she found all but one. Nobody, however, knew anything about the raid.

"Someone is holding out on you," I said. "Probably more than one."

"I'll get to the bottom of this, Major," she said.

They covered their tracks pretty well.

"You will have to let this thing take its course," the Minister advised, "or the public will say it was stopped because you had been mayor of Saint John."

I agreed, but the trial was perhaps the worst experience of my life.

I knew I had done nothing wrong and wasn't worried about the outcome. I thought the worst I would have to bear was the humiliation. Then two of the witnesses began to lie: the SCS and the office girl, who, I had been told, was in the plot, along with the two young men from the Department of Health and the programmer/acting manager, who started it all. (The

Preacher was not a witness—they couldn't find him! Long before the trial started he had cleared out for the west coast.)

The Commission's lawyer must have thought they had a pretty weak case nonetheless, for instead of dwelling on the canteen cheque and the hay deal, most of the questioning was about an invoice concerning my car, an equally flimsy charge easily cleared up.

The jury found me not guilty.

Afterward the RCMP officer who had conducted the raid told me and my lawyer the name of the person who had called them to do the search; and another man came right out and said that the Preacher had called a friend of his, a lawyer, for information on how to get the RCMP to do the search and take his evidence.

The Mounties also told me and my lawyer that they couldn't find anyone, beyond those who brought the case, who had a word to say against me.

A bad situation had ended as well as it could and I went back to the farm with only one or two sour notes to follow: five people lost their jobs as a result of my acquittal, but they were not people of consequence among my enemies; and a large invoice was tendered to the Board for legal services re: advising the Board on legal proceedings against E. A. Flewwelling, and attendance at a preliminary hearing. That invoice was paid out of the farm budget!

Since the farm had paid legal expenses for the Board, and since their charges had proved false, I asked that my legal expenses also be paid. But it was not customary … individuals … bad precedent!

I went back to the farm because I enjoyed the work I did there, but not before I had made it clear to the Chairman of the Commission that I had had my fill of the SCS; of the interference of inexperienced people with more book-learning than brains; and with the cheeseparing of the Commission in financial matters. I went back with promises from Fredericton and a 40 per cent raise.

CHAPTER NINE

The Acting Managers

WHEN I WAS TOLD TO STAY HOME TILL the whole thing was over, Duke left the farm, but the SCS sent for him and offered him the foreman's position at a good salary.

"On one condition," says the Duke.

"And that is?"

"You bring back the Major."

So the Duke was away from the farm while I was suspended, but other residents called every day to pass on the news.

According to them ... the Preacher helped himself to the men's prescription drugs, which he shared with his wife. Then the two of them would get into such a state somebody would have to drive them to the Regional Hospital for a shot and then take them home again, where they would sleep till noon ... the Preacher's wife spent a lot of her time hiding from her husband in the residents' bedrooms.

... The Preacher gave away the farm library (a large collection of books that had been donated to the farm by the library at the DVA Hospital) to the Westfield School, leaving the residents without good reading material.

... After he paraded the two farm horses in front of the barn, he paid a man to shoot them and haul them away for dog food. (Satan was not there; he had been sold. And Jack had passed on by then.)

... He did away with the storeman's position and moved all the groceries to the basement under the kitchen, eliminating the controls I had in place. Then he sent his son to the basement each morning to pick up canned goods for the family's meals in their trailer home.

... He took a lot of farm tools with him when he left, saying that he had loaned them to the farm; but everyone knew that he had come with only a few clothes and a borrowed trailer.

... When he left, leaving many unpaid bills behind him, he tried to take the borrowed trailer. (It took the owner, a police officer, the sheriff, and a lawyer to stop the CPR from loading it onto a flatcar bound for Vancouver.)

Not bad for less than six months as acting manager. But he forgot that other people could see right through him. They were all sober then, and they were better witnesses than most, for "it takes one to know one," and a career on the booze gives a man unlimited opportunities to observe human nature at its worst and to learn, if not to practise, the skills of deception and fraud.

When the Preacher had cleared out, the newly constituted permanent Commission sent Big Shot to take his place as acting manager.

Big Shot was an out of work party supporter, but he puffed himself off to the press as a busy man who had taken on the extra responsibility simply to help out the Chairman. Actually, they owed him a favour.

If the Preacher had been a rogue, Big Shot was a trial. It was enough to make me long for the halcyon days when Bill and Annie were bickering in the kitchen and there was nothing worse to deal with than a few invoices going for payment more than once.

Big Shot sold all the cattle for $2000 and thought he had made a great business deal. There were 21 head, three of them milking, the rest all beef animals in good condition worth about $1000 apiece.

When I had been reinstated and started on the rampage about the fine herd I had been building up over the years, Big Shot told the Chairman of the Commission that there had been no one to do the milking. (So he sold all the beef cattle!) In fact, there had been at least five men from farms in residence.

Moreover, the Big Shot claimed that he put on a long rubber glove and turned a calf in the womb so it could be born!

"You know about as much about cows as I know about

flying airplanes!" I stormed. "You've been watching too much TV. There were no calves born at Lonewater while I was away."

The day I came back to take over the farm, at the request of the Chairman, Big Shot was all ingratiating welcome as he showed me what he had been able to accomplish. He was no tornado—but a messy little wind all the same.

"Made a small improvement in the Manor House," he confided, as I hung up my coat. "Yes. Returned 21 pair of skates that your first A.-M. ordered. Never even out of the boxes. All there, too, except for the three pair he took with him. So I said, 'Better we had something we could use in place of these things,' and I took them back. Couldn't expect cash for them, but, of course, I think you'll like what they gave me in exchange."

All the time he was puffing out this little speech, Big Shot was leading me up the spiral staircase and into one of the best rooms in the house. There, as self-important as its purchaser, stood a handsome, brand new double bed.

"Now, I had the room done up so we'd have a place for anyone from the Commission who cared to stay the night," he said, "but it occurred to me as we were coming up the stairs just now, actually, why couldn't I stay here while I'm in the city? You know I'm moving on to the Detox Centre on Hazen Avenue from here? Yes ... acting manager ... just to put the place on its feet, you know ... be very convenient for me ... of course, we wouldn't have to say anything about this little idea of mine. No need to tell the tax man what he doesn't need to know, eh, Flewwelling?"

From Hazen Avenue (once he had that centre thoroughly confounded) Big Shot moved on again, this time to Commission headquarters in Fredericton as head of finance, where his first act was to direct that the farm driver pay $100 a month board, and all staff $1 for each meal. The total cost to keep a man on the farm at that time was $1.65 a day.

As head of the financial department, Big Shot hired Noisy.

One day the Manor House door blew open to admit a man who announced himself to be the new purchasing agent, working under Big Shot. Everything, henceforth, was to be bought through him.

Noisy started out by calling the farm's best suppliers and swearing and shouting at them that their prices were too high and their deliveries too slow.

I learned about this attack on the farm's friends (those who, besides giving the farm their best prices, used to send presents at Christmas and ice cream in hot weather) when they started calling me to find out who this loudmouth was who thought he could curse and swear at everybody.

"Call the Commission," I told them. "We didn't hire him. He was palmed off on us."

But Noisy was smart enough to get all the local suppliers so mad they wouldn't sell anything to the farm anymore. Then he took his business to friends in Fredericton.

He bought meat from a large wholesaler (where his wife worked) without going to tender. When I questioned him, he said he had asked for prices from a stall in the City Market and from a retail store in Moncton and found that prices at the wholesale plant were by far the best.

"Big deal," I said. "That took a lot of figuring." But sarcasm went right over Noisy's head.

Big Shot's shadow fell across other events at the farm as well: road building for example.

Ducks Unlimited sent an engineer to talk to me about building a dam on farm land across Goose Creek, to raise the water and give more nesting places for ducks. An access road across the farm would be necessary.

I agreed but wanted the road built so that traffic could be seen and controlled from the office. Big Shot, however, without telling me, directed that the road should run through the woods out of sight of the farm.

When they were ready to begin the road, the engineer hired some of the residents and the farm tractor to clear the route of trees and bushes. Lots of willing hands signed up. These men didn't often have an opportunity to earn a little for themselves, and so they worked like good fellows and got the job done.

But a week went by, and no pay. When I inquired about the delay the engineer replied, "those cheques were sent to Fredericton."

"Why didn't you give them directly to the men? They are all here."

"I intended to do that," the engineer replied, "but Mr. Big Shot came down from Fredericton and ordered me to send all the cheques to him."

I picked up the phone.

Big Shot blustered but eventually backed down and agreed to mail the cheques to the farm.

They arrived, and every one of them had been endorsed on the back "For Deposit to the Account of the Alcoholic Commission," and an enclosed note directed the recipients to "Sign on the back and return to Big Shot. Replacement will be issued."

I was disgusted and advised the men to refuse to sign the cheques. I wanted to charge Big Shot with tampering with personal documents, but the men wanted their money and they signed.

A few days later the replacement cheques arrived—each one minus a tax deduction.

That man was one of the meanest, smallest men I have ever met, and I have met thousands.

Needless to say Big Shot's choice of route for the road backfired like everything else he did. He had his way; the road was built out of sight of the farm buildings; and people went down it after dark and stole potatoes.

One day I arrived at the farm to find Big Shot there, all puffed up as usual. He was waiting to meet the new programmer for the province, who was expected that morning. When the car was seen in the drive, he rushed into the office and began going through the books as if he were the auditor, just like a frightened kid trying to impress the school bully.

Then the new man walked in, and I didn't know whether to laugh or cry.

IF THE PREACHER WAS A ROGUE and Big Shot a nuisance, this man was a bad joke. They called him Mouth.

As soon as I saw him, I recognized him. Here was the same man who, less than two years before, had called my office and asked if I could see him on Saturday. He had just been appointed to run a farm for alcoholics in Nova Scotia (eight residents on 18 acres) and he wanted to know how to manage the place.

I took him mentally, step by step, through the operation of Lonewater and gave him copies of the standing orders. We spent all Saturday afternoon together and part of Sunday. Now here he was, come to give advice and direction.

Mouth's visits kept up once a week for about a month. Then I went to Fredericton, got hold of the Chairman, and announced, "If you want to see what Mouth's profile looks like, just let him come to the farm once more and it will be in the wall where I will be putting him."

"That bad, eh?"

"Worse."

"I'll keep him away from you," the Chairman promised.

Mouth came only once more to the farm, for twenty minutes a few years later—with my permission. He came to trade a chesterfield that belonged to his mother for a load of hardwood for his fireplace, both to be delivered at the Farm's convenience when the truck was going to Fredericton.

IT WAS BIG SHOT WHO SHUT DOWN the woods work at the farm. He decided, all on his own, that the residents should not be going into the woods; or, conversely, that somebody from Fredericton should be going there instead. From then on the boys at the farm split firewood only. But they became the largest volume supplier of stove-lengths and fireplace logs in the Saint John area, so Big Shot stopped them from buying hardwood from the local people and gave a contract to a man outside Fredericton.

When the trucks first came in, I did the scaling. The supplier didn't like the scale. I had scaled for my father from boyhood; and when the farm had been sending pulp to Irvings, I had scaled every load, and in a whole winter's cut there had never been more than half a cord's difference between my scale and Irving's.

Big Shot called and asked me to go easy on the scaling. I replied, "There's only one way to scale and that's the right way."

After that the wood came in the evening after I had gone home.

The farm needed a bookkeeper and I was asked to find one. This I did and submitted the man's name to the Commission. The candidate was a retired Mountie who had also been a chief of police in a suburb of the city. He was well qualified as a bookkeeper. He was also a great worker in his church, especially with youth and seniors, and he was interested in the job: he wanted to work with the residents of Lonewater. Pretty hard to fault a man like that.

"Where does he live?" Big Shot asked.

"On the east side of the city," I replied. "About 20 miles from here."

"Oh, dear, dear, no. Much too far," and he proceeded to appoint someone from Fredericton, which, as everybody knows, was 50 miles away.

While he was at it, Big Shot came down and, without telling me, transferred all the money in the farm's bank account in Saint John to the account of the Commission in Fredericton. Then he closed the Saint John account and deleted my name as a signing officer. Lonewater had $60,000 in that account, money the residents had earned toward the expenses of running the farm.

His motives were anyone's guess. Did he suppose somebody was going to dip into the till? Surely not! At appropriate intervals the farm's earnings had always been paid over to the Department of Health, and the auditors had always been satisfied.

Did he think it a slur on the dignity of the Commission to have an institution under its umbrella actually making money? Surely not! Maybe he just thought it would be more efficient to have everything macro-managed from his office. Or perhaps he wanted to add to the empire the Commission was building.

In any event, having already put an end to my frugal management by appointing Noisy as sole purchaser for the farm, Big Shot went on to cause me acute embarrassment at the bank and endless aggravation from then on.

I nearly started a trade school at the farm. Through

Unemployment I arranged for a teacher from the Westfield School to come evenings to help residents to higher levels of general education. And through the Community College, I found a man willing to come and teach welding, and another to teach cabinet making.

Big Shot got wind of this plan and threw up his hands. Oh, no, no! I had no right to make such arrangements on my own. Teachers coming to the farm? Dear, oh dear! This must be negotiated through his office.

A few days later I received two phone calls, one from the Community College and one from Unemployment. Sorry but Mr. Big Shot had made it impossible for them to participate in the plan for the farm. They were very sorry, but they would have to call the whole thing off. They couldn't work through that dummy in Fredericton. He wanted rent for the room, yet! What kind of idiot was he?

I could have answered that question fully, but it would have taken too long. I contented himself with saying, "Any kind you like."

It can be said that I never suffered fools gladly. But I can also say that, gladly or any other way, I suffered a great many during those middle years at Lonewater, but none more insufferable than Big Shot.

CHAPTER TEN

Lonewater Miss

NOISY TOOK OVER THE BARN, THE BARN the residents and I were so proud of. Without warning, I received a memo stating that Noisy would be in charge of the barn and that box stalls would be constructed to house racehorses. Noisy had connections with the racing community.

I immediately telephoned a friend at Commission headquarters. Unfortunately, my friend had learned to toe the party line.

"So," I growled, "Noisy is going to let his friends use our barn. Is he going to feed and clean their animals?"

"No. He will keep the present barn man on."

"But the barn man is a resident!" I exclaimed. "He's getting along fine and will soon be ready to leave."

"Noisy will determine when he leaves."

"And when did Noisy qualify as a counsellor?"I demanded.

"Noisy will manage the barn."

I was livid. "And cut the hay and haul it in?" I barked.

"The men at the farm will do that when Noisy wants it done."

"Then why not let Noisy take over the farm?"

Click. End of conversation.

NOISY HAD HIS WAY and racehorses began to arrive at Lonewater. Each one stayed up to several months, depending on the reasons for its being there. Mares in foal stayed longest and were always objects of interest to the residents. Rarely was there a man so hardened he couldn't feel awe and delight at the sight of a foal's first steps beside its mother, or amusement at the antics of those lovely little creatures when first led out to grass.

The racehorses were a pleasure for the residents.

A mare and her foal, of course, stayed together. Everyone knew that, but one morning Lonewater Miss, about four months old then, was separated from her mother when someone accidentally shut them in adjoining pastures. Seeing her mother across the fence, the foal panicked, jumped, and came down on a steel post that tore a terrible gash deep into the upper part of her right hind leg.

She lay on the ground shuddering, and the men who were nearby stood stunned, gaping. Duke came running from the barn, his face drained of colour.

Once across the fence, he walked slowly to the foal's head and sank on his knees beside her. Eyes dull, ears laid back against her neck, she stared straight ahead. He murmured to her softly, and laid the tips of his fingers on her neck.

She tried to jerk away.

Still speaking softly, he reached out again.

This time Lonewater Miss lay still and allowed the man to touch her.

The Duke turned to one of the residents. "Warm water," he whispered. "And we'll have to move her inside. Bring the sled."

At that request, the men scattered for water, a blanket, and the sled. I received a phone call at my home and I instructed the counsellor to call the vet, as well as the owner of the colt. It would be a blow to him; he had high hopes for Lonewater Miss.

The Duke stayed by the foal's head, stroking her neck and murmuring to her. When they brought the water, he slowly moved toward her leg and began to bathe the wound. Lonewater Miss closed her eyes and lay still.

When the bathing was finished, the Duke and a couple of men wrapped the foal in a blanket and with the help of the others very gently moved her onto the sled and into the barn. She had stopped shivering, but her ribcage barely moved.

I arrived at the farm as quickly as I could.

"Major?"

I shook my head.

"The bottle, Major. You know, with the nipple. And more blankets."

"Water? In the bottle?"

"Yes. And in a bowl. Warm water and antiseptic. And a softer cloth."

"Duke, I had the counsellor call the vet."

"What for!"

"Duke, it had to be done."

"But you know where that leads."

I knew. But I had no choice. The Duke could forget inconvenient facts; I couldn't.

When the bottle came, the foal swallowed a little water.

"Come on, then, Duke," I said. "She's warm and she's had some water. That will help combat the shock. Come in the house. We can wait for the vet in there."

"You go," Duke said. "I'll stay here."

"You know what will have to be done, Duke."

"Over my dead body," Duke muttered.

In his mind Duke was back on an Italian battlefield. They

Lonewater Miss, soon after her birth at the farm.

had found a little filly there, suffering from gunshot wounds. They called her Princess Louise after the honorary colonel of their regiment, the 8th Hussars. That little princess recovered. This little princess would recover too. He'd see to that.

"Never mind, darlin'," he whispered. "Don't listen to what the Major says. We nursed a princess back to health in Italy, and I was only a sergeant then. I'm a duke now. That ought to count for something."

When the vet and the colt's owner came, they just looked at Lonewater Miss, shook their heads, and backed toward the barn door. A leg wound in a horse … poor little thing.…

"So when can we expect this to happen?" Duke growled.

The owner turned a blank stare on him. "Well … whenever you want to do it, I suppose," he said.

"Whenever I want to do it? It's not my job to shoot your horses for you."

The owner raised his hands.

Duke looked him over. "You want me to shoot your horse, do you?" he rumbled. "Well, I'm sorry but I don't think I can do that. Not till next week. At least next week. Maybe the week after. We'll just have to see how she goes."

The vet looked confused. "But we can't leave her like that," he said. "It will have to be done immediately."

"Well, I can't do it."

"I beg your pardon. If you have time to care for a wounded horse, then you have time...."

"Never mind that."

The vet looked at the owner. The owner shrugged. The vet shrugged, took a firmer grip on his bag, and followed Duke back into the box. Not knowing what to say to each other, the owner and I listened to a running disagreement, politely expressed, over the stitching that was going on inside the stall.

After a few minutes, the vet came out of the box, walked out of the barn, and drove away.

I leaned into the box. "Duke?"

He was talking softly to the foal.

"How does it look, Duke?"

"Great. Marvellous. A beautiful piece of stitching."

That didn't sound right somehow.

Then Duke came out and put his hand on the owner's shoulder, steering him toward the door. The owner looked back once or twice but allowed himself to be put into his car and started on his way.

"That turned out better than I hoped," I said.

"Sure did!" Duke said cheerfully. "Now call the vet."

"Call the vet! Duke, he just left!"

The Duke was already walking back to the barn. "Not that twit!" he snorted. "Call a good vet."

"What's the problem?" I argued. "I thought you said he did a good job of the stitching."

"He did, for making aprons," Duke growled. "This is horseflesh."

I still stood in the barnyard.

Duke turned back. "Look," he said, "I told that so-called vet to stitch the inside. Deep inside. First. Then the next layer. Then the next. And to leave the skin open. So the wound would close from the inside out. But did he? No. He just pulled the skin together. So it has to be done over again. Then I can put the salve to her, and she'll be fine inside a week."

I went away and called another vet, one who said equine medicine was not his line so he would take Duke's word for it.

But the miracle didn't happen inside a week. For three weeks the Duke lived by the foal's side. Every two hours he applied salve. And he fed her, and cleaned her, and crooned to her. Often early in the morning I would find him asleep in a straight-backed chair in a corner of the box.

But Lonewater Miss grew stronger. Her wound healed from the inside out. The scar was no wider than a line drawn with a pencil; we had to look for it to see it. And as she recovered she began to play again. When Duke fell asleep in his chair, she would sneak up behind him and blow on his neck. He would start awake and shoo her off. And she would dance away, circle around, wait for him to fall asleep, and wake him up again.

Lonewater Miss never had to be broken to harness. She and Duke were such friends, she accepted the bridle from him without any fuss at all; and when she was ready for the sulky it was natural to her to do whatever he asked.

She followed her mother to the race course after all, and in her first year won twice, placed twice and came in to show once. Many evenings the recreation hall rang with cheers as the men followed her career on the radio.

The Duke's personal race was not so easy. He was one in a million, but he lacked self-esteem.

Shortly after the cattle were settled in the new barn, he told me that one of the cows was sick. He thought it was mastitis. Her nose and udder were hot, and her milk was lumpy. I went out to the barn and agreed with Duke's diagnosis. "Yes," I said. "Looks like mastitis. I'll call the vet."

The vet arrived, examined the cow and confirmed the diagnosis.

"That's what the Major thought," Duke told him.

After that the Duke told everyone I sure knew cattle. "The

After an amazing recovery thanks to Duke, Lonewater Miss went on to a Maritime racing career.

Major said it was mastitis, and that's just what the vet said."

I took him aside. "Duke," he said, "I didn't say what was wrong with that cow. You did. I just agreed with you. You told me what the cow had. Duke, you know more about cattle than any of us on this farm. I take your word for whatever you say is wrong."

Duke thought about that a long time, and over the course of many years came to see the truth of it. Saving Lonewater Miss (and many other successes as well) also helped him, and in the end, he, too, came in a winner.

CHAPTER ELEVEN

More $4000 Buildings

WHEN I FIRST WENT TO LONEWATER Farm in October 1968, there were for human habitation, besides the Manor House, a cottage (called Jeffrey House at Annie's request in honour of someone dear to her) and the Farm House, which had been the home of the foreman from time to time in the farm's balmier days. Both were in pretty bad shape.

Nine years later, the Farm House had been vastly improved at an expenditure of only $5000 and housed 13 men. Jeffrey House housed 12 men, after improvements costing $4000. About $3000 had been spent on the Manor House, which housed 15. McLaughlin Hall, a wholly new and modern kitchen and dining facility that seated 80 men in comfort, had been built by the men; value, $40,000. Carten House, which housed 14, had been built for a little over $4000; value, $30,000. And Peters House, which was used as a hobby centre before it, too, became a residence, had been reclaimed from down the road and was worth $15,000. In nine years Lonewater Farm had grown to be called a village at a total cost (1977 dollars and including the new barn and wagon shed) of $140,000.

In spite of trials and tribulations, in spite of bureaucratic interference, in spite of budget cuts and too many "experts," the farm had grown, projects had been completed, and residents had gained self-respect and confidence.

"CARTEN HOUSE—Constructed the building from the ground up out of second-hand lumber and factory-reject pressboard on interior walls and reject plywood on exterior walls. The house is two storey, heated by hot-air furnace, has seven bedrooms, a washroom and toilet on the main floor, a laundry, shower, and toilet room in the basement, also a large lounge. This building houses 14 men." (My notes)

In 1973, when Carten House was built (just after the barn was finished) the farm desperately needed more accommodation for the men who were applying to stay there, but the Board felt the cost would be too great.

Carten House housed 14 residents.

"We have lots of lumber left over from the barn," I told them, "and windows that I picked up at the same time. I'm sure the cost would not be higher than we paid for the barn."

But that was a barn. Could the residents build a house? A house was a different kettle of fish. For a house you needed an architect. There was an architect on the Board. What did he think?

Oh, no. The architect didn't believe I could site the building or work out the contours for the basement. After all, I was proposing to build into a side-hill.

I assured him that my men and I could do both. "Just leave those problems with me," I said.

As I had done for the barn, I proposed to build from a

model, not from drawings. Well, all right. But the architect would have to approve the model. Agreed?

I waited for a really rainy day. Then I drove to the city, parked a block from the architect's office, walked in the rain to the office, and said, "I'm parked on Prince William Street. I have the model in the trunk, but it's too heavy to carry. Would you like to come down and see it?"

The architect looked out the window. "Tell me about it," he said.

I explained the chalet style, how the house was to be set into the hill, what it looked like from various angles."

"Floor plan?"

I described the floor plan.

"Okay."

Carten House went up for a little over $4000. On the main floor (upstairs, because of the site) there were six bedrooms. The basement contained a furnace room, laundry, and bathroom, at the back; and at the front, where windows looked out on the river, two bedrooms and a recreation room. The recreation room had two big picture windows (salvaged from a store on Main Street) and a door leading out onto the lawn.

When we finished Carten House, we held a big open house. That was November 3, 1973, a calm, sunny day, and 200 people came.

As the cars drove up to the gate, a resident welcomed the guests and handed out pamphlets about the purpose, plans, and history of the farm. Two men on horseback led the way to a field where the cars were parked. The rest of the men showed the guests the houses, barn, and shops. The kitchen crew served tea, coffee, sandwiches, and cakes in the Manor House. And the Lancaster Kiwanis Steel Band played in the sunporch. It was a great day and good advertisement for the Farm.

The Minister of Health came the day before the opening. He said he was sorry he couldn't come on the day but he could do more for us in his office anyway.

"And I can do more for you when I have a crowd," I said.

Then we built McLaughlin Hall. Since it was a kitchen and dining facility, McLaughlin Hall cost a bit more than $4000, but it was built entirely by the men at the best possible price.

The Lonewater Hitching Post for October 18, 1974, says:

"The past few weeks have seen a great deal of progress being made on the construction of McLaughlin Hall, which when completed will serve as a modern new kitchen and dining area at Lonewater Farm.

"The hall is named in honour of the late Dr. John McLaughlin, a pioneer and great friend in the circles of alcoholism in Saint John and New Brunswick.

McLaughlin Hall served as the kitchen and dining facility.

"Under the careful guidance of [a resident] the outside siding was finished just over a week ago. At the same time [another resident] oversaw the task of installing a complete electrical system.

"On the inside [a third resident] assisted in finishing up fibreglass insulation.

"A water-based heating system is expected to be completed in the near future."

November 5, 1974, saw seven and one-half yards of cement poured to finish the basement. During the week of November 30, N.B. Power installed the needed increased power supply. And *The Post* for December 14 reported that the heating system, though not yet functional, had been installed, and that the acoustic tile ceiling was also finished.

The middle of January 1975, saw the opening of "Peters

House." At first it served as a paint shop and additional hobby-craft shop. Later it was renovated and had a small kitchen added. It then consisted of two large bedrooms, a small bedroom, toilet room, large lounge, and sunporch.

"Peters House" was a gift from Art Peters of Westfield, a friend of mine. It had to be moved, that was all.

Like many landowners along the river, the Peters family were building a new, year-round house where there had been only a summer cottage when Westfield was mostly a summer resort. Many of those summer houses came down in the '70s, but the Peters cottage was going to be cut into two or three pieces and moved to Lonewater.

The Duke and I went to Westfield to look at the job and decided we could haul the building on skids behind the truck. But first we needed two tractors to move the sections to the road.

Over the next little while, the farm readied itself for the move. The Department of Transport gave permission to use the highway. The day came. And I sent a crew to bring home the house.

The first section came off its foundation posts without a hitch, passed through a narrow gap between the new house and the neighbours' fence, and approached the edge of the highway when along came the RCMP.

At that moment Duke was driving up in the old panel truck that had gone over a culvert and never been the same again. When he saw the police he didn't stop. But, rethinking his decision, he turned and came back.

As soon as he stopped, the officer walked over and asked what he was doing on the highway in a vehicle in that condition: one headlight missing, one door off, hood bent, windshield cracked ...

"I was just down at the garage to get the vehicle repaired," Duke said, "but I forgot to ask the Major how much he wanted to spend." The police and chronic alcoholics fight a running battle, and to the alcoholic, cops are fair game.

The officer grinned. "You're a good liar," he said. "I saw you go down the road and turn around just a few minutes ago.

You tell the Major to keep that thing off the road till it can pass the test."

"I'll do that," Duke agreed with an equally friendly grin.

During this exchange, the other Mountie was talking to the driver of the truck. "You can't move a building onto the road on skids!" he said. "Where are the wheels?"

The driver leapt out of the truck. "My God!" he hooted. "Don't tell me they fell off!"

Peters House first served as a hobby shop then was renovated as a small residence.

So they left the section of cottage by the side of the road and went back to the farm. "Major," they said, "the cops won't let us move the building till we have a big set of wheels under it, like moving contractors use."

I called every contractor in the city, but it was Saturday afternoon.

"Well," I said, "I'll call Art Peters and explain the situation. We'll just have to wait till Monday."

Sunday morning at seven, my phone rang.

"Coming to the farm today, Major?"

"I always come on Sunday. Why the early call?"

"It's all here, Major!"

"What's all here?"

"The house! While those damn Mounties were snoring in their beds, we got up and moved the whole works!"

They were all in on it. Even the cooks got up in the middle of the night to make breakfast.

CHAPTER TWELVE

They Said There Was Drinking

IT IS HARD TO UNDERSTAND WHY THE COMMISSION wanted to stifle all this vitality and turn Lonewater Farm and its residents inward on themselves, but that is what they achieved over the course of a decade or so.

In fairness, Dr. Chalmers may not have known everything that went on. He was very busy, and the men he chose to have around him probably kept him in the dark. On one of Big Shot's periodic visits to the farm to announce another hair-brained scheme, I asked, "What does the doctor think about this?" "Oh," Big Shot replied, "the doc doesn't know! Uh-h.... Have you ever seen his appointment book?" The fact remains, however, that few public officials have even assembled a more inept, inefficient, insensitive set of men as Dr. Chalmers did. Quite a feat for an out-of-the-way place like New Brunswick!

They said there was drinking at the farm.

I replied, "There are always those who will come to the farm seeking help but not really ready for it, and for the first week or so their desire for a drink is so strong they will find a method of getting a bottle to the farm—taxi, friend, or a trip to town. We have 950 acres to check, while buildings with one open door, such as the Provincial Hospital and the Detox Centre, have drinking problems. When these problems no longer exist we can do away with the farm and other such centres."

They held workshops and seminars at which they presented papers to each other on the statistics of the alcoholism problem and on the latest theories for combatting it.

After sitting all day at one of these meetings, suffering a mixture of boredom and amazement, I stood up.

"What do you know," I asked (and everybody heard me) "about a man that is down and out, and drunk? Have you seen him try to stand, and fall down, and cut his face? I have. Have you seen him throw up and beg for a drink to settle his stomach? Have you handled a man in the D.T.s, when you had to call in four strong men to hold him down till he came out of his terror and agony? I have. Have you ever had a man ask you to hold him—literally hold him—and not let him go to town to get a drink, crying while he tells you he needs that drink? I have held such men."

There wasn't a sound in the room.

"When you can answer 'yes' to those questions, gentlemen," I continued, "then you will have a basis for forming theories and methods for rehabilitating alcoholics. Our method at Lonewater keeps them active, at work that requires some concentration. In time they realize they can function without a mind-altering drug. We help them find out what they can do sober. We give them a chance to enjoy their minds and muscles, sober. We treat them like men, not numbers.

"I've talked to alcoholics," I said, "who have been in hospitals and treatment centres. 'Those psychologists,' they say, 'in they come every two hours to give you some pills and a lecture.' It drives the men crazy. They tell me that after a few days of that all they want to do is go for a good drunk."

Then I walked out.

I knew what I was dealing with at Lonewater. I never believed the farm's healing environment would take instant effect or that it would heal every man who went there. Quite the reverse. I expected all manner of stratagems to get hold of a bottle, and I tried to anticipate them. When I failed, I dealt with the situation immediately and firmly.

One nice bright day in January, when the men were assembling for lunch, one of the woods workers reported to Duke that some of the boys were enjoying themselves out by the old log.

Duke knew exactly what that meant. "We better take a walk out the back woods road, Major," he said. Not far into the woods, we began to hear singing. The Duke looked at me; I waved my hand to indicate that we should carry on quietly.

Two men were sitting on a big log singing like a couple of blue jays. The other one was standing in front of them conducting.

"What's going on here?" I barked.

The concert stopped abruptly, and almost in unison they replied, "Nothing. Just singing."

"It's a nice day, isn't it, Major?" one of them added.

The Duke strode forward. "You two stand up," he ordered. "Now, what did you do with the bottle?"

"We haven't got one, Duke."

As quick as a flash, Duke turned, grabbed the conductor, and extracted a bottle of wine from his inside pocket. He hadn't been an army sergeant for nothing.

"Now," he said, "let's get to the kitchen. It's time to eat."

He handed me the bottle and I carried it back to the farm, bringing up the rear behind Duke and his three "prisoners."

When we came into sight of the kitchen, the others were all lined up waiting for the cook to open the door, and to a man they turned and watched the Duke and me herd the choir across the snow, nearer and nearer.

The parade halted within a few feet of the lunch line. Then I handed the bottle to its owner and said, "If you three want to eat, then empty that bottle on the ground right here."

The man hesitated, but not for long—just till the Duke stepped up beside him and growled, "Now!"

To the cheers of those lined up for lunch, the bottle was drained onto the ground.

"Get in the line and eat," I said. "Then see me in the office after lunch."

Because those men were new and it was their first offence, I gave them a good tongue-lashing and let them stay. Later they all thanked me, and the Duke, for that action, and became model residents.

Three men of the First Nations transgressed in a similar way, but their outcome was not so happy.

They had been at the farm long enough to know the rules and the consequences of breaking them. Yet on one of my frequent walks into the woods to see how the pulp cutting was going, I found them sitting around their fire, but without a tea can on. As I approached, one of them tipped up a bottle, took a drink, and passed the bottle to his neighbour.

I stepped into the clearing. "What's going on here?" I demanded.

"We are having a little fun," one of them answered.

"Not here," I said.

One of the others looked up at me. "You don't belong to our tribe," he said. "We're Micmacs."

"No," I said, "I don't. I'm Iroquois. Now you leave your saw and get out of here. I'll see you in my office. Get!"

I don't know whether it was the threat of having the Iroquois down from Cognawaga that moved them or the big German shepherd at my heels, but they got.

They had to turn in their bedding and leave the farm. They knew better.

One day I found the storeman intoxicated. I had him taken to his room, then returned to search for the bottle. But it couldn't be found.

What could have happened? Well, the spread sheet said that a case of six bottles of pure vanilla had been delivered. Sure enough. Nothing but an empty box. Vanilla will give a man as good a drunk as rum, except that the feeling doesn't last as long.

The storeman was reassigned and the wholesaler advised not to take any more orders for pure vanilla. That storeman was not dismissed from the farm because, through no fault of his own, he had been placed in temptation's way. He just had to start all over again to straighten himself out.

My army of walking wounded was not made up of the "average patient" of the Commission's statistics: of fairly intelligent, fairly robust, fairly young men only, who just happened to have a single problem. Many of them had been through the wars, literally and figuratively.

One man arrived who had an old-fashioned wooden leg. After a few days, when he began acting a little tipsy, he was searched for pills. They were in the wooden leg.

A nice old fellow from the North Shore came to the farm.

They called him Frenchie. A real gentleman and one of the neatest cutters in the woods. One day he went to town and didn't return when expected. Relic, who had been sent to the city to pick up oil, spotted him on the street. From Relic's report it appeared that Frenchie was just lost in the big city. Relic told him if he wanted help to call the Major. Frenchie replied that he didn't have any money so Relic gave him enough to use the phone.

Relic himself, who was generally reliable, got into trouble that same day. Somehow he had a couple of drinks, and on the way home, driving along Douglas Avenue, rear-ended the car ahead of him. He spent the night in jail and the next day was remanded to my care.

One evening, when I was staying late, I received a call from

The Farm House was a residence for 13 men.

the Farm House that "the Doctor" was sick. The Doctor was a retired dentist who was in his 80s and not in good health when he arrived at the farm.

I went quickly to the Farm House and found the Doctor stretched out on a couch.

"How do you feel?" I asked.

"I'm dying," the Doctor replied.

"I'll have your dinner brought over," I suggested.

"No. Just something to keep me warm."

The old man looked bad.

"Somebody bring a blanket," I said, "and call Dr. McLaughlin and a priest."

Then I sat down on the couch beside the old man and tried to rally his spirits while waiting for help to arrive. But the only reply I ever got was, "I tell you, Major, I'm dying."

Still trying to humour him, I said, "Well, then, die like a soldier with your boots on."

With that the Doctor took a deep breath and fell across my lap, just as the priest arrived.

I tried to resuscitate him, but Dr. McLaughlin entered on the heels of the priest and pronounced the old man dead.

When everything requisite had been done for the old man, I walked back to his office to call the Doctor's son. I hoped the son wouldn't be like the daughter I had to call on another such occasion. "Don't send the body here," she snapped. "You got it. You look after it."

Or the family of the young man who came from the Provincial Hospital with pills hidden in his clothes. One morning just before breakfast, his roommates caught him with a handful he was just about to swallow, and took them away from him.

"You can't do that at Lonewater," they told him. "This is a place for getting over pills, and booze, and stuff like that."

"I know," he replied.

"You all right?"

"Yes. Just give me a few minutes. You fellows go on to breakfast."

When they returned, their roommate was stretched out on his bed. One look and they knew he was dead.

I called the doctor and the coroner; the body was removed to the Provincial Hospital; and the people there informed the father, whose name was unknown to me.

A couple of hours later someone from the hospital called back, half disgusted, half amused. "Major," she said, "you're in big trouble now. That young fellow who died? His father is going to sue you!"

"Oh, yes?" "Because I didn't call him myself, at once, I suppose."

"That's it!"

"Did this father tell you why his name was not on the

documents that came to the farm with his son?"

"Oh, we already knew that! He didn't want anyone to know his son was in the Provincial."

"And how many times did this father visit his son in the hospital?"

"Humph! Never!"

"If he cares that much about his son, tell him to sue. I'd love to get him in court."

But of course he never did.

All this went through my mind as I walked slowly back to my office to break the sad news to the Doctor's son. "It's a good thing," the son replied. "He wasn't much good for anything anyway."

It had been a long day and I had just lost a resident. "He was your father," I barked into the phone. "Maybe he would have done better if he hadn't had you."

CHAPTER THIRTEEN

The Ghosts of Fire

ONE YEAR BETWEEN CHRISTMAS AND NEW Year's a group of residents of the farm visited my home to see the family tree and sample some of Mrs. Flewwelling's Christmas baking.

As they were sitting comfortably in the living room with tea cups in their hands, the phone rang. "Major, the garage is on fire!"

Everyone left the house in a rush, but we were too late. Even the Westfield Fire Department had been too late. The garage was nothing but a frame, and Relic, near to tears, was standing beside the truck (which had not been inside) mourning the loss of the tractor. A chain dangled from the front of the truck.

"I could have saved her," Relic howled. "I had the chain hooked to her, and she was coming out fine, fire and all, but that—Counsellor. That—Counsellor, who don't know a tractor from a hole in the ground ... he come running up and ordered me ... ordered me, to stop. 'Unhook that chain!' he hollers. 'Unhook her. If you pull her out here, she might blow up ... blow up, Major! She was a diesel! I could've saved her! I could've saved the garage!"

I submitted a full report to the Commission and had a reply from the Chairman himself, wanting a guarantee that there would be no more fires at Lonewater.

I rang him up. "Good Lord, Doctor," I said. "I can't guarantee that you will live to get home from your office!" "The hell with it," the Chairman growled.

If a guarantee had been possible, it would have been a good thing, for on Wednesday, May 7, 1980, in the early hours of the morning, the Manor House burned to the ground.

Fire destroyed the Manor House in 1980.

The ruin was heart-breaking. That house was one of the finest examples of the early architecture of this province, as well as the administrative centre and physical heart of Lonewater Farm.

One of the counsellors, making his regular nighttime rounds, spotted the fire, but the men in the house had already been roused by the smoke and were hurrying out. They lost everything. The Duke even lost his army medals.

Everybody tried his best to fight the fire, but it was a hopeless task from the beginning: the house had been constructed with a clear draft between the studs from the basement to the attic and insulated with birch bark. So when the fire started in the basement wiring—there was no holding it back.

And as if the house had decided to end it all, the first part to burn was the telephone connection, and somebody had to drive pell mell to the nearest house, about a mile and a half away, to sound the alarm. Neighbours came, and fire departments from both Westfield and Grand Bay, but there was nothing they could do to save the old house; they concentrated on preventing the fire from spreading.

I rushed to the scene as soon as I was called and suffered the night through with the men. I could see the flames even before I reached the Westfield Ferry.

Perhaps the old house had simply had enough: Glasiers, and Coffins, and Hazens, and the rest: wood cutters, and tramps, and the Alcoholic Commission. The gone-but-not-forgotten Preacher had bought wall-to-wall carpeting for the bedrooms. Wall-to-wall carpeting in a house like that! And he had nailed the 200-year-old shutters together and cut holes in them to install new windows! Worse vandalism than painting the mahogany doors and making off with the antique mirrors.

ANNIE CLAIMED THERE WERE GHOSTS in the old house. Just before she left for Halifax to move her furniture, knowing that I would be staying alone while she and Bill were away, she asked him if I believed in ghosts.

"No," I replied. "No. Why do you ask?"

"Because this house is haunted," she said.

"No!"

"Well, I was wiping up the hall floor one day when a man walked past me and went into the living room," she said. "I told him to go on in and I would be with him in a minute. But when I went in nobody was there."

"Probably went out through the sunporch," I suggested.

"No. Wintertime. Windows were shut."

I didn't say anything more and headed for my office, but Annie followed me there.

"One night," she said, "I had some ladies in to play cards, and a French sailor walked in."

"A French sailor?"

"Yes. A French sailor. I knew by the cap he had on. One of those knitted ones with a tassel over his ear. He came in, leaned his arm on the mantle, and bent down to look at the television where I had it standing in the fireplace. "What's wrong?' I said. "Have you never seen a television before?"

"The ladies all looked around. "Who are you talking to?" they said.

"Just then the sailor vanished. None of the ladies saw him."

"I have never seen a ghost," I said. "I hope I will, but I don't believe one will show itself to me."

"If you don't believe in them, you won't see them," Annie told me.

There was a ghost in the house the time somebody brought a couple of walkie talkies onto the farm and set one up in the lounge, where they all knew Donnie Monk liked to relax in the evening after he finished in the kitchen. He would grab the paper, settle himself in an easy chair, and read as a way to wind down after the day.

One evening they turned the lights out, and when Donnie started down the long, dark hall, a ghostly voice whispered, "Donnie … Donnie … I wa-a-a-ant you."

Donnie came running out of the house as white as a ghost himself. "There's a ghost in there!" he shouted. "The place is haunted. Help! Help!"

Donnie refused to speak to the boys for several days after that. Stories like these were often retold by the boys who liked nothing better than to reminisce. Eddy might ask, "were you there when little Beamer come back to the farm for Christmas? Not that Beamer was a ghost. But now he's sort of the ghost of Christmas past, as you might say."

"No-o, Eddy. I don't remember anybody called Beamer. How did he get that name?"

"Well, I'll tell you …"

"Beamer, it seems, went through the farm programme more than once, if the truth is told. But he'd always drift back to his old ways. One day, near Christmas as the Major's driving along, he sees old Beamer standing outside the liquor store on the West Side with his hand out.

"The Major parks and gets out.

" 'What are you doing here, Beamer?' he calls out.

" 'Just greeting my friends, Major,' says Beamer. 'Just greeting my friends.'

" 'You don't greet your friends with your palm up, Beamer,' the Major says. 'You greet them with an open hand. You don't need to beg. You're getting welfare money. Go get yourself a clean room. Wash up. You'll feel like a new man.'

" 'Thank you. Thank you, Major,' says Beamer. 'Have a good day.'

"Well, sir, the very next morning when the Major gets to the farm, who does he see but old Beamer standing there waiting for him.

" 'Beamer!' he says. 'What are you doing here?'

" 'You told me to get a clean room,' says the Beamer, all smiles. 'So here I am!'

" 'But how did you get here?'

" 'Walked.'

" 'All the way from town?'

" 'Yep.'

" 'It must have taken you all night!'

" 'Did. In fact, as you might say, Major,' says Beamer, 'I'm clear tuckered right out.'

So they let him stay. After all, he was almost one of the family.

"Oh, yes, Beamer stayed—and bunged up the housekeeping something awful! My God, yes. Will I ever forget!

"You see, just about this time it happens that light bulbs start disappearing from all over the farm. Fellows would leave their rooms to go to work, or dinner, or take a bath—whatever—and when they come back ... total darkness! Not a light bulb in the place.

"Now it's Christmastime, you recall, and one evening the Beamer says to Duke and one or two other fellows, 'Come and see my Christmas tree. That young Indian, there, Hiawatha, he cut it for me—nice young fellow, Hiawatha—and it looks real good now I got it decorated. Done it all myself.'

"Yep! That's what happened! Duke and them go up to see Beamer's tree and lo-and-behold-you, as my old grandmother used to say, hasn't it been Beamer that's pinched all the light bulbs. And not only that, but he's painted them all different colours out of old paint cans he found somewhere. Funny thing was, it looked real nice.

"So that's how old Beamer got his name. Light bulbs. Beams. Lights. Beamer. Get it?

"Poor old Beamer. The boys used to tease newcomers that

didn't know him. 'You go and ask that big fellow over there,' they'd say, and there would be only Beamer—five foot two if he was a inch, and muscles like a ten-year-old girl.

"One time he got awful mad at Duke for some reason. Forget what happened now, but Beamer was fair frothing.

" 'That Duke just better watch himself,' he says, 'for if he don't ...' and he puts up this fist that's about the size of a shrivelled walnut.

" 'Beamer,' says Duke, 'if you ever lay a hand on me and somebody tells me about it, I'll be very cross.'

Now you talk about mad!

"Oh, yes. Duke could get a man going. But I never heard anybody carried a grudge about it."

"No, no. Fer he only meant it in fun."

"One time Sundown was wandering around looking lost and Duke says, 'What are you doing, Sundown?'

" 'Just looking for something to do, Duke,' says he.

"So Duke says, 'Change your boots and get ready to unload a carload of corn flakes.'

"Well, Sundown goes back to his room, meets a fellow there, and says, 'I don't know ... what kind of boots do you wear unloading a carload of corn flakes?'

" 'Well, I don't know either,' says this other fellow. 'Are you going to be using a shovel?'

"THAT DUKE! REMEMBER SMOKY? Little fat guy? From Moncton, I think it was ..."

"You mean the little guy that used to work in the barn?"

"That's right. Smoky. Liked the cows, and goats.... Wanted to be like Duke...."

"Duke used to play with the billy goat, you see. He'd hold Billy's horns and pat his neck, and then, quick as a flash, he'd grab his legs and lay him down on his back on the ground.

"And the goat would keep coming back for more.

"That's right. Billy'd jump up, rear up on his hind legs for a minute like he was hopping mad; then he'd down with the horns and make a run at Duke all set to knock him into next week.

"And Duke would laugh, and they'd play the game again.

"After awhile Duke would turn his back on Billy and walk away. And Billy would watch him go as much as to say, 'Well, there he goes. The game's over for this time. That's life, I guess.'

"So one day Smoky thinks he's friendly enough with the goat he can play that game with him too.

"They was right outside the cellar door to the Farm House, you see, and it open. And when Smoky turns his back to walk away, Billy there, butts him so hard on the seat of the pants, he goes flying half way across the basement floor and fetches up against the furnace.

"Fair shook the house down!"

"THAT YOUNG FELLOW, HIAWATHA, that you mentioned. Now there was a good looking kid, and you couldn't ask for a nicer one. But 19, and already at the farm. He must have been drinking since he was knee high. It's a wonder he ever got through school. But he did."

"Yes. Terrible chip on his shoulder at first...."

"Hiawatha stalked into the Major's office the day he arrived, and the first thing he said was, 'I'm an Indian.'

" 'I know,' says the Major. 'Where were you born?'

" 'Burnt Church.'

" 'All right. You're a smart, good-looking young man with a grade-twelve education. Is Burnt Church in New Brunswick?'

" 'Yes.'

" 'Is New Brunswick part of Canada?'

" 'Yes.'

" 'Then,' says the Major, 'you are a Canadian.'

"Hiawatha thought for a minute. Then he looked the Major straight in the eye and said, 'Yes!'

" 'All right, then. You are the same as all of us here. All Canadians. So go and ask the big man you'll find in the hall what he wants you to do. His name is Duke.'

"That young Canadian was a good worker and tried hard to overcome his addiction. And when he left, he thanked the Major for the help he had received and walked back into the world with his head up.

"One rainy day not long before he left, when he was spending time in the hobby shop, he made a beautiful leather tie. The pendant had an Indian chief's head painted on it, and the slide that tightened and loosened the tie bore the painted head of a pretty Indian girl. Hiawatha took it to the Major, placed it around his neck, and said, 'It's for you.'

"The Major really prizes that gift."

I TOO HAD STORIES TO TELL and one of the most rewarding was about another 19-year-old. A lad from down St. Stephen way turned up. They called him simply "Boy," because he looked so young, which helped him to fit right in with the kids when I ordered him back to school.

Nor was Boy in favour of going back to school at first.

"Well, you'll go," I said, "and your mother will be proud of you."

"Huh!" says Boy. "I haven't seen my mother for years—except once, when she came to visit me in jail."

"Well, then, I'll be proud of you," I told him. "And so will Duke and all the men." I took Boy to the School Board office and made arrangements for him to go to vocational school.

After that, Boy went away to school every morning. Somebody would drive him to the end of Campbell Road, where he would wait for the school bus with all the other Woodman's Point kids, and pick him up there again in the afternoon.

Boy's going to school made Lonewater even more of a home to the residents, and they were all proud of him. As long as he lived among them, Boy went to school; and if he hadn't a mother, he had 50 uncles all pointing out to him the value of education.

After he left, the uncles often wondered how he was doing, and they were greatly satisfied a year or two later when an invitation came in the mail for me to attend the graduation ceremony at the Vocational High School in the city. Of course I went, and I was as proud of Boy as I was of my own three sons.

CHAPTER FOURTEEN

The Private Army Comes to an End

EACH YEAR AFTER I REACHED THE AGE OF 65, I received a circular letter from Big Shot in Fredericton, advising all older employees of the Commission of the advantages of retirement, and hoping that they would avail themselves of their heaven-sent opportunities. I could just see Big Shot's fingers all crossed at every joint, but I never took the bait. As I received each letter, I called my friends in Fredericton and told them I wasn't ready to retire just yet. In this way three years went by.

I was hoping to be at the farm to see the new office completed, for the design was partly mine. But when three years had gone by and there was still no new office, I found out from a counsellor that Joe Boy had said, "When the Major goes." I felt I was holding up the progress of the farm. I had better retire.

I realized that the Commission's "professionals" would never agree with my methods of rehabilitation, and that I would never agree with their agenda of giving lectures. They were convinced that AA meetings weren't the answer, and I could see that my support of AA was in vain.

I thought it over and told my staff that the time had come for me to climb some other mountains. By this time I was serving my second term on the City Council, and I knew that I would never need to be idle. I would miss the farm and the men. I would even miss the constant skirmishing with Big Shot and Co. Nevertheless, time was on their side, and I set December 30, 1986 as the day.

On the evening of the 29th someone from the local office of

the Canadian Broadcasting Corporation phoned.

"Major," he said, "it has just come over the news wire that tomorrow you are retiring from Lonewater."

"That's right," I said. "I will be through tomorrow after 18 hard, trying, but happy years."

The next morning I drove to the farm to do a day's work as usual, but I had only finished my rounds and settled down in my office when a reporter arrived from the Saint John *Evening Times-Globe*.

Talking to this man and showing him the farm took up a lot of the morning, and I was just about to suggest a cup of coffee when two television vehicles, from different networks, drove up. "Gentlemen," I said, "all I'm doing is retiring!"

"It's a big day, Major," they assured me.

When lunchtime came, I invited all the media people to join me and they all trooped into the dining hall. The TV reporters, as it turned out, had always intended to stay; they already had their equipment set up. But it was a surprise to me.

McLaughlin Hall was packed. Besides the media, there were all the residents and all the employees of the farm, and the wives of the employees; there were people who had been farm employees in the past, with their wives; there were employees from Ridgewood; there were many ex-residents, some who had left the farm years before; there were AA representatives, and my own family and personal friends. The only people who hadn't come were the crowd from the Commission.

There was much talk and well-wishing, words that I felt very moving. I particularly remember one lady saying, "Never mind, Major. They didn't come from Fredericton because they knew they would never have a retirement send-off like this."

The cameras recorded the activities, the presentations, and the speeches. "A day like this makes it all worthwhile," I responded. Then, because the media were there, I gave them a few of my favourite observations.

"Over the years, I have worked with full responsibility for the farm and the residents. My aim has always been to continually improve the place and the physical and mental condition of the men. I have instilled in my staff and in those residents who held responsible positions the same aim and desire and spirit of loyalty. And I have not been disappointed.

"Lonewater has been an unusual place. For one thing, it has been the only provincial institution that has made a financial return from its activities. Lonewater has generally paid most of its costs. I remember a year when we earned $130,000 and one when the province had to lay out only $7000 for our support.

"Lonewater has worked because we have embraced the concept of giving each man the gift of being treated as a valuable individual no matter what his background or lifestyle may have been.

"We have had men come here directly from Dorchester Penitentiary, where they had been sent for alcohol-related crimes. We act as a good half-way house for them, where they can finish their sentences while learning how to fight the addiction that got them into trouble in the first place.

"We have always told these men, 'Nobody here will know where you came from unless you tell them yourself. As far as we are concerned, you are a resident just like all the rest. You have already seen that there are no bars here and no guards to stop you from walking out if you want to. If you do, of course you can't come back, and you know what the alternative would be. But if you start down the drive, nobody will stop you.' I am proud to say that not one man has ever left here before his time was up.

"Many of our residents arrived at the farm thinking only of themselves, but by the time they left they were thinking more like responsible citizens. From the very beginning this was one of our aims.

"I see many faces here today of men who have been through our programme. They are men who have turned their lives around. They have learned to like positive, productive sobriety. Lonewater, I am proud to say, has an enviable record of success. I salute our successes. Sobriety through productivity. There are no hopeless situations, only men who have grown hopeless about them."

There was a ripple of laughter mixed with the applause. All

the residents, past and present, had heard these final words, not once but many times.

SO THE BOYS FINALLY GOT RID OF THE MAJOR—and missed one of the social events of that eventful season.

It is interesting to remember that my years at Lonewater were almost exactly contemporaneous with the tenure of the Hatfield government in Fredericton. And everybody who remembers the night the political map of New Brunswick went Liberal—red from end to end—will never forget the send-off they had, or the scurrying from the sinking ship immediately afterward.

The new government, holding every seat in the Legislature, stamped out its predecessors root and branch. Included among the casualties was the Alcohol and Drug Dependency, Commission. It was to have been a great Commission, not unlike the Electric Power Commission. It is no more.

Today I am too busy climbing other mountains to fret over the battles I won and lost while managing Lonewater Farm. But I do often think of the Farm.

Perhaps a battered panel truck passes me on the road, and I recall the day they moved "Peters House."

The old van was in bad shape by then, and Duke knew he shouldn't have it on the road. It hadn't been in great shape even before Annie sold it to the Province along with the farm. It had remained road-worthy until the day some of the residents were reporting back after shopping in town. It went out of control and ended up nose-down in a deep ditch, with its rear-end hung up on a culvert. Four men had been sitting in the back; without warning they were all in the front seat with the driver. Nobody was hurt, but the van was never fit for the highway again.

In the days before that accident, when it was still possible to take the van out on the road, it developed a weakness in the door catches at the back. The doors would fly open at unexpected, and sometimes inconvenient, moments. You just never knew.

There was the morning Mr. X had what they thought was a heart attack.

"Lift him mattress and all," I ordered, "and we'll take him to the hospital in the van."

The driver, three residents and I moved like lightning and took off, almost literally, for town.

"Call the city police and get us an escort," I shouted to the clerk as he slammed the door and gravel spurted from behind the tires.

God bless them, a police car was waiting when we reached the city line at Grand Bay, and by the time the cavalcade swept down on the toll bridge we were moving right along.

The police roared through the barrier and the van after them.

That was when the back doors flew open, just as a commissionaire erupted from a toll booth and tried to give chase. The men in the van took great delight in airing their spectacular vocabularies through the opening.

It was probably all the commotion that caused Mr. X to start up, just as they were topping the bridge, and cry out, "Boys, I'm dying. Get me my beads out of my pocket."

"Too late to turn yellow now!" said the Cat, who had accompanied us.

Mr. X lived, and a great time was had by all.

IN SPITE OF THE VICTORY I HAD WON for alcoholics needing treatment in general hospitals, I had trouble with hospitals from time to time. I once took a resident to the city who needed better care than they could supply at the farm—and these were men who didn't run to the doctor with every little hangnail. This man was sick.

Eventually, a woman in crisp white with a smile as crisp as her pant suit informed us that the resident would be admitted.

"Good," I said. "That will be a relief to the counsellors at the farm. They are not trained to look after very sick people."

"Of course," the female person said. "Well, let me see ... this is May 27th. We'll have a bed for him on the twelfth of July."

"Very good," I replied. "Where will I have them put the box?"

With another crisp smile, "What box is that, Major?"

"The box this man will be in by the 12th of July."

They admitted him a week later.

THE FARM HAD TWO TRUCKS besides the van. One came with the farm from Annie; the other was bought. When we started cutting pulp we needed a bigger truck than Annie's one-ton, and the Duke and I went to town to buy one, if we could find a bargain.

As we drove into the yard of a dealer who was going out of business, a farmer also was driving in with a two-ton Mercury he wanted to trade, now that there was a sale on.

I enquired the price. The dealer said "Oh, I could let you have that for $2,200, seeing it's for the farm." Everybody tried to look unimpressed, and the Duke, who had driven many trucks, sauntered over, kicked a few tires, glanced in the cab, and came back and whispered to me, "Low mileage, and she's only two years old."

Then I looked the truck over, and kicked a few tires ... well," I said, "all right. But I'll have to ask you to hold it for me till tomorrow. You understand I'll have to clear the purchase with my Board."

I went home and called every member of the Board (This was in the days of the Foundation—before the Commission) but the President was in England and the others were all out of town. Frantically, I called Dr. Carten. "Ed," I said, "we have to have a truck. I've got a deal on one, but everybody is out of town. You'll have to back me at the next meeting."

By this time Dr. Carten's questions were routine. "You know what you're doing," he said, as always; and I went back to the dealer and bought the truck. After that I had a hydraulic hoist installed and went into the business of hauling pulp to the mill.

They hauled pulp not only from Lonewater but also from other farms in the area, so that in six months, when the Board met again, I hadn't a qualm.

"Who authorized you to buy a truck?" they started in. "What powers do you think you have? Do you expect us ...?"

When they had just about run out of words, I said, "Now, gentlemen, if you will turn to the next page of my report, you will see that the truck paid for itself in six months."

"Hm-m, yes. Well! Interesting. Shall we move on? Next item?"

ONE BRIGHT MORNING IN SPRING, when Mill Brook was running just under the deck of the bridge and the truck was returning to the farm, Bonehead jumped off the back into the water.

Knowing that he must find help fast, the driver pushed the accelerator to the floor and kept going toward the farm. As soon as we heard, the Duke and I roared back in the old panel van and plunged along the course of the stream, me on one side, Duke on the other.

The brook was flowing fast and yellow, over its banks, swirling among the alders that grew along the summer course, slipping over smooth pans of ice in the stream. At times we had to wade.

I spotted Bonehead first. He was on Duke's side of the water caught in some bushes.

"Duke! On your side!" I shouted over the noise of the stream. "In that clump of alders just ahead of you!"

"I see him!" Duke shouted back.

Duke waded into the water waist deep, cursing Bonehead with all his fluent command of the language.

"If you want to drown yourself," he roared, as he hauled the victim out, "do it on somebody else's property!"

Bonehead went to Ontario a few weeks later, once he had replaced the glasses that remained in Mill Brook.

PERHAPS THE OLD VAN'S FINEST HOUR came on the second of February, 1986, when the Groundhog Day Gale wiped out southern New Brunswick.

There was no power in the region (in some places not for many days) and most people were without heat or any means of cooking. All the residents except the kitchen crew took the trucks and worked around the clock clearing downed trees from power and phone lines. The van's part was to round up all the young children and seniors living around Woodman's Point and take them to McLaughlin Hall where the kitchen crew could keep them safe and well fed—the farm kitchen used propane. It was a lark for the kids and old folks, and a definite lark for the men.

I couldn't reach the farm till the day after the gale. By that time Duke was running a hot soup delivery service up and down Campbell Road and around Woodman's Point.

"You're supposed to be visiting your daughter!" I exclaimed.

"Too many kids and old folks to be fed and kept warm for me to be visiting family—much as I would like to," Duke replied.

IT IS NOT TO BE SUPPOSED THAT ANY OR ALL of the residents drove the farm vehicles willy nilly. Only a few had that privilege. Since he was foreman, Duke drove at need. Relic, being very good with vehicles, was a driver in the early days, but he was more of a tractor man and did less and less driving on the roads. It was Big Mo who grew into the driver's job and kept it.

Big Mo turned up at the farm as a resident in 1974. At that time, he was down and out. When he had been there for a while, he mowed a lawn for a lady in the neighbourhood and was delighted with the six dollars she paid him.

After that he never looked back, and by 1980 he had become official driver for Lonewater, a civil servant. He was honest, loyal, and reliable, and he held that job until he was ready to retire.

Big Mo always lived at the farm and saved every penny. In 15 years he had saved $100,000, bought a new car for cash, and retired a relatively wealthy man, all because, as he said, "the Major trusted him."

CHAPTER FIFTEEN

The Pole Fence

VERY EARLY ON, I HAD A CEDAR POLE FENCE placed around part of the pasture, which greatly improved the farm's appearance from the lane.

When the Board visited just afterward, the President remarked, "I hope no animal leans against that!"

And another member said, "It looks pretty, but I don't think it will last very long."

The fence was still standing straight and strong 18 years later, even though it had been leaned on quite a bit.

One animal that often leaned on that fence was a pony called Bandit, who liked cough drops. I had learned better than to give ice cream to horses, but forgot myself in the matter of the cough drops.

Bandit ran up to the fence one morning to find out why his friend was making strange sounds and smelling funny. I gave him a cough drop and had one myself. And the rest, as they say, was history.

Maybe Bandit was too short to jump the fence. Maybe he wasn't as independent as Satan. At any rate, he stayed in the pasture, but he developed a chronic bad cough from that day forward, which, strangely, affected him only whenever he saw me coming. We used to lean on the fence together, coughing and eating cough drops to our hearts' content. And the fence never even creaked.

The fence was standing when I left. So were many of Lonewater's "graduates," straight and tall—and still are.

The Mechanic arrived at the farm about the time they acquired another old truck, this one from the government. Both Duke and I lighted up when we heard about him, but to make sure he was good, Duke put him to work on a couple of lawnmowers.

When he had done a great job on the lawnmowers, they led him to the old truck.

"How much to fix this and get it roadworthy?" I asked. (A mechanic in town had wanted $1,700.)

The Mechanic took half an hour or so, then wiped his hands on an old rag and said, "$200."

"Right. Get started!" I ordered.

That truck worked in the woods and even delivered pulp to the Irving mill for about two years.

The Mechanic had a dual addiction, alcohol and drugs. The drugs were in his system for a long time. Twice he went berserk and had to be taken to the Provincial, but eventually, after a couple of years, he was well enough to leave and live with his mother.

Then we heard that he had been killed in a car accident, and everyone was very sorry.

But about three years later, one morning when I was mowing my lawn at home, a car drove up and out jumped the Mechanic.

"Major," he said, "I want you to meet my wife and our new baby."

All three were good looking and healthy.

The Mechanic said with pride that he hadn't taken any alcohol or drugs since he left the farm and that he was running his own business. That day he was taking his wife of nearly two years for a short trip to show off the baby.

I was proud of that family.

Other men started their own businesses after being at the farm. One, who had been drinking since his school days and continued till he finally sought help at 50, left after three years with the confidence and strength to set up as a landscape contractor. For the rest of his life he did well and remained sober.

Another left to become a supplier of coffee makers to offices and businesses. He soon had several people working for him.

A third became a welding instructor. He needed three stays at the farm to finally win and become a productive citizen, but he did it. The Cat was another. He was a carpenter. They called him "Cat" because Duke saw him nearly fall off a ladder but save himself by some fancy footwork. "He's like a damned cat, that guy!" Duke said. The Cat landed on his feet in life, too.

Many other residents found jobs and stayed sober for the rest of their lives after leaving the farm. Over the years, now close to 30, I have received any number of letters and phone calls from them to report progress and express thanks. While Duke lived, they always asked to be remembered to him as well.

Duke passed away a few years ago in his early '70s. Many alcoholics ruin their health and die young, but Duke's great strength of body and generosity of mind lasted out the allotted three score and ten. He had to fight long and hard against the bottle, but he won in the end and spent the last five years or so of his life in his own apartment in town, where he stayed sober and enjoyed his family and many friends.

Having a supportive family was an important factor in Duke's recovery. However heart-sore she may have been at times, his daughter never deserted him, and other members of his family followed her lead. They are proud of his memory now, and I am proud that Duke's daughter not only allowed me, but was happy to allow me, to use her father's true name in this narrative. Elton Langille was the Duke's real name. The names of most of the others have been suppressed, mainly because families are ashamed to have it known that one of theirs has been in the Provincial, or (horror of horrors) been through a rehabilitation program.

Duke arrived at Lonewater only a day or two after me, and one of the first tasks he had to perform was attendance on a man who went into the D.T.s. I recognized Duke's potential from the first, but that incident was a severe test for both of us. New on the job and without medical help, I was afraid I was about to lose my first resident; and holding down a companion in such horrible agony and then sitting with him afterward was very hard for a man who was just coming off a drunk himself. But we both survived the ordeal, as did the sick man, and we gathered strength from the fact that we could do it.

Duke spent about 18 months at the farm the first time. Then he told me it was time to go to town and get a real job and make a new life. I was sorry to see him go, but the point of Lonewater was to prepare men to re-enter society. I reminded Duke, "Keep in touch." About six months later, Duke returned. He had failed to stay sober. This pattern was repeated several times. Duke would feel he could succeed out in the world, and a few months later I would find him drunk on the street or hear that he was drinking in some rooming house in town. Then I

A rare photo of Duke, at left, with the Major, centre, and another gentleman.

would go and get my old friend, hold him under heavy security for a few days, and put him back to work.

In the final years, after I retired and the Duke was living in town too, we used to see each other frequently and talk over old times. Then the conversation rarely touched on the alcohol problem, but always on the fun.

Duke had been a woodsman from an early age and often relived the days when he was foreman of the woods crews at Lonewater. One of his favourite stories was the one about Nut and the Swede saw—Nut didn't stay long, but he made a deep impression.

"I see by your record that you are a woodsman," I said to Nut at his first interview. "We could use a good cutter. How are you with a chain saw?"

"Never use one," Nut announced. "Always use a Swede saw."

Now a Swede saw is a metal-framed, hand-operated saw invented in Sweden. Before chain saws came along it was in general use, but not any more.

"I think we have one on the place," I said, "but it is very slow compared to the chain saw."

"I can cut as much pulp in a day with a Swede saw as any other man with a power saw," Nut replied. "Give me eight blades and I'll show you."

When the Duke came in from the woods, I told him the story but said, "Try him out. Give him an area near you, and let him use the Swede saw. It can't do any harm."

"Nut!" was Duke's only comment.

But the next day he took Nut and his Swede saw to the woods and gave him a pile of logs to saw up into four-foot lengths.

"We'll have the pot boiling about ten o'clock," he said. "Come along then for a cup of tea and let me know how you're doing."

Nut set to work with his Swede saw and cut up a tree or two. Then, saw in hand, he walked through the woods till he came to the place where Duke had been cutting with the power saw. Actually he and his crew hadn't accomplished much that morning, and at that moment he was filing the saw. But they had a sizeable pile of pulp in their clearing, most of it cut the day before.

Nut spied the pile. "Did you cut that this morning?" he demanded.

"Yep," one of the helpers told him, "but the saw isn't working too good today."

"To hell with this!" Nut muttered.

With one hand he threw the Swede saw as far as he could in among the trees and took off running.

He was never seen again.

Duke knew all about my troubles with Fredericton, of course, and another of his favourite stories was about the road Big Shot wanted to build but didn't.

I may have had to retire from the battle before it was finished, but I had won my share of skirmishes, and the road was one. (This road was not the one to the dam that Ducks Unlimited built but a proposed widening of the lane that led from Campbell Road to the Manor House and the Nerepis.)

Big Shot was determined to build an in-and-out road of standard width to replace the lane. I was determined that it wouldn't be widened. I argued that a wider road would encourage people to drive down to the farm at all hours. I pointed out that the farm had only one driver; that a wide road would destroy good land; that they damn well didn't need a new road! But I knew all the time that arguing with Big Shot was like whistling in the wind.

Big Shot arranged for government engineers to survey and mark out the road.

"All right," I said to myself, "this is a question of power. You won't get your road without a fight."

I called the Minister of Environment whom I knew well. The plan, I said, would spoil a lot of good land and forest for nothing.

"Don't worry," said the Minister. "It won't happen."

But the very next morning Big Shot called. Engineers from Sussex would be along in a day or two.

I called Sussex. Had they heard anything about the road job being cancelled? Yes, they had, but they were going to walk the route anyway—to keep the Commission happy. Just walk the route. They wouldn't survey it or stake it. The road would not be built.

On the day the engineers were to come, Joe Boy, another of Big Shot's clones, arrived on orders from Big Shot. Without informing me, he took the crew off the wood yard, where they were sawing and splitting stove-lengths, and ordered Duke to sharpen stakes for laying out the road.

Well, the engineers came and they all started out to walk the route, through swamp and pasture, woods and plough land—Joe Boy with his conscripts carrying his stakes, the engineers just sauntering along.

After they had tramped some way through the woods off Campbell Road, Joe Boy began to flag and to wonder when they would be starting the work so he could catch his breath.

"When will we start placing the stakes?" says he.

"Never," says the senior engineer.

Joe Boy blinked once or twice, sneaked back to his car, and drove off. The rest of them strolled up to the farm for coffee and a good laugh.

AS LONG AS DUKE LIVED, he and I got together often; and busy as I am, to this day I miss him. I also miss Eddy, the storyteller.

Eddy was very fond of Dr. Moar, who also liked to joke and tell yarns. One day the doctor came into the Manor House singing a little army ditty. It was a lovely day, and he was spreading his good-humour all around.

That day Eddy was first in line to see him. He was already sitting in the patient's chair.

The doctor walked in singing, set down his bag, settled himself in his chair, grinned at Eddy, and kept on singing till he had finished the song.

Eddy leaned across the desk and whispered, "Doctor, you wouldn't have any more of your pills would you?"

Eddy had the doctor going another time, too, when they first met—maybe that was why they became such friends.

Eddy was a reader, and I recommended to him a book about somebody's adventures sailing around the Horn, which Eddy enjoyed enormously, so much so that he soon had it pretty well by heart.

One day, before he knew his man, Dr. Moar made the mistake of asking idly, "What was your line of work, Eddy?"

"Well, Doctor," says Eddy, "most recently I was a gardener in the city, but in my young days I went to sea."

"Oh, yes? That's interesting."

"Yes, sir. Sailed around the Horn...." And Eddy proceeded to give the doctor chapter and verse from the book.

"That's an interesting fellow," the doctor told me later. "Did you know he'd been around the Horn in his youth?"

A real old-fashioned gentleman arrived for help at the farm. He was a black man, well known to many of the residents and well liked by them. His name was George.

George had badly mutilated hands and everybody tried to help him, but he was very independent. He would leave the dining room after each meal with the other residents even though, as the cook informed me, he hadn't eaten very much.

I went to George's room to have a talk with him. Always polite, George stood up when I entered, offered me a chair, and said he was pleased to have me visit.

In answer to questions, George said that he left the dining hall with the other men because he didn't want to hold up the kitchen crew. I therefore arranged for him to start his meals a half hour before the others and for his food to be cut into manageable pieces. At breakfast time, though, he would stay longer so that neither he nor the cooks would have to get up earlier than usual. George appreciated this kindness very much.

Now George and Eddy became friends, two old gentlemen together, and one day Eddy went to see me distressed almost to tears.

"I've done it this time," he said, "and I'm so embarrassed. I feel terrible."

Knowing Eddy, I expected to become the butt of a joke, but he went along. "Well, what happened, Eddy?" I asked.

"Well, you see, Major," said Eddy, "George's niece bought him a record player and a few records, but they're all those fast, modern things, so I said to George, 'George,' I said, 'what are you playing that kind of music for? That's not the kind of music for old fellows like us.' 'What is our kind of music?' says George. And I says, 'Oh, you know. Old Black Joe. Stuff like that.' Major, I feel just awful."

"And what did George say?" I asked.

"Oh, he just laughed."

Eddy was so full of stories the Major never knew whether he made them up or they really happened. He liked to tell Eddy yarns just to hear him come back with another one. There was one about a girl with a wooden leg—Eddy claimed to have begun his dancing career with her. And then there was the girl at the bowling alley who was a little behind—she had split the seam of her slacks hurrying into her bowling shoes (she was a little late) and didn't appreciate Eddy's innocent remark.... The stories were endless, and now that Eddy has passed on, I remember most of them and tell them for him.

Eddy and I shared a birthday, and till Eddy died in a nursing home, I never failed to visit him on that date.

SO THEY SAID I WAS UNPROFESSIONAL, an out-of-date old bungler so stiff-necked you couldn't tell me a thing, so impractical I honestly thought I could make a difference by getting involved. Making friends of old bums and derelicts, for God's sake!

In their view there was nothing to be done with old reprobates like George and Eddy. The whole lot of them ought to be recycled, if the truth were told—though one had to go through the motions. There was really nothing to be done except to give them their pills and try and din it into their sodden heads that they were useless to themselves and everybody else but BUT ... if they would only have horse sense and listen to what the latest studies showed ... if they would only have horse sense enough to listen, they might improve themselves and maybe recover a little self-respect, though the Lord knows....

Just like that bunch of old idiots to put up a fence around their blessed pasture and expect it to stand! Here's George, this post here. And here's Eddy. And Duke. And all the rest of them. There they go, marching around the pasture like a bunch of bloodied infantrymen from an army in retreat. Talk about your walking-wounded! They looked like they'd fall down any minute. *Only they didn't.*

Why didn't that damn pole fence fall down!

Well, because I believed in my fence, and in my army. Involved, was I? So be it. I thought more of poor Pigman, who cried when piglet died, than I did of some other people I knew. Which of those fine, straight poles did they think was Pigman?

More drugs to control drugs was not my way. Jawing at a

man who would do better if he could, and was doing as well as he could, was not my way. And though I retired before the battle was over, I knew that the war was not won.

At that time, drugs to control drugs was the wave of the future. Now it is the wave of the present, and each new drug that shows promise is hailed with rejoicing. The wave of the future now, however, looks different; it looks like a return to my methods. At least the latest treatment for teenage drug addicts is communal living, personal responsibility, and return to school to build up self-esteem and to prepare for a productive future.

What goes around, comes around (in rehabilitation circles as well as everywhere else) probably because nobody really knows what alcoholism is, how it finds its victims, why it succeeds with one and not with another, or, in the end, how to heal its victims when they cry for help.

Two men arrived at Lonewater. They were both painters, both good painters, both nice fellows when sober and, at least as far as anyone could tell, both determined to go straight. One left to become owner of a manufacturing agency with three employees. The other rented a room at the Ten Eyck Hotel and burned the place down. He ended up in Dorchester. Who could have anticipated either outcome?

An era has ended. "In Tempestate Floresco / We Thrive in Adversity."